I0891787

# POLKINGHORNE

# POLKINGHORNE

## INSIDE THE TRIAL OF THE CENTURY

STEVE BRAUNIAS

ALLEN&UNWIN
AUCKLAND • SYDNEY • MELBOURNE • LONDON

First published in 2025



Note: Quotations and details from the trial are all available for public access on the court records.

Allen & Unwin Aotearoa New Zealand
Level 2, 10 College Hill, Freemans Bay
Auckland 1011, New Zealand
+64 (9) 377 3800
auckland@allenandunwin.com
www.allenandunwin.co.nz

83 Alexander Street
Crows Nest NSW 2065, Australia
+61 (2) 8425 0100

EU Authorised Representative: Easy Access System Europe,
Mustamäe tee 50, 10621 Tallinn, Estonia, gpsr.requests@easproject.com

A catalogue record for this book is available from the National Library of New Zealand.

ISBN 978 1 99114 240 5
Cover photo: David White, Stuff Limited
Design by Katrina Duncan
Printed and bound in Australia by Opus Group

10 9 8 7 6 5 4 3 2 1

MIX
Paper | Supporting responsible forestry
FSC® C001695
FSC www.fsc.org

To Mark Braunias
(20 August 1955–17 December 2024)

*Steve, I am sorry to hear about your brother.*
*Please accept my condolences.*
Text from Philip Polkinghorne, 21 December 2024

# Contents

# Contents

He was grateful that however uneasy the rest of his life had turned out to be, it had once contained enough peace to give him pleasant dreams; and he often suspected, with more than a little righteousness, that this might be what kept him essentially more stable than his wife.

— *Revolutionary Road*, by Richard Yates

INTRODUCTION

# The Legend of Polkinghorne

His name was Polkinghorne. Polkinghorne, first introduced to the nation as 'a person of suspect', as he put it in his typically anxious and mangled English; Polkinghorne, whom the police quickly suspected of murder and then slowly, not altogether competently, went about investigating the amazing, very distracting, and apparently criminal extent of his sex life, finally arresting him for the murder of his wife Pauline sixteen months after he made a 111 call on the frantic morning of 5 April 2021, saying she had hanged herself in their strangely impersonal white complex above a beautiful shining lagoon on the mansioned eastern slopes of the Auckland isthmus; Polkinghorne, acquitted and let free to wander the Earth by a jury at the close of an epic, shockalicious eight-week murder trial like none before it in our island history — and surely none after it, unless some other surgeon or likewise high-earning urban professional, whose hobbies include hookers and methamphetamine, is accused of something so diabolical that it's of an even lower moral order than murder, Polkinghorne, that long, drawn-out, perky, improbable name, became a kind of household brand in the winter and spring of 2024, something everyone recognised and regarded with a mixture of rage, awe, wonder, fascination, scorn, distaste, zero sympathy and close to 100 per cent actual downright hatred; Polkinghorne, those three syllables thrown together almost at random, forming a name that will remain fixed as a garish icon in the psychic territories of the New Zealand mind, will achieve a sordid immortality but an immortality nonetheless, supernatural and haunting. Say his name three times into a mirror and you might see him suddenly appear behind you, small and enthusiastic, a blue-eyed voodoo doll, a demon of wealth and white privilege hopping up and down on his madly socked feet — Polkinghorne, Polkinghorne, Polkinghorne.

I got to quite like Dr Philip Polkinghorne. We chatted constantly in an upstairs courtroom at the High Court of Auckland during his murder trial that began in July and ended in September of 2024. I have interviewed people accused of murder quite a few times — including a Chinese guy who killed two men with a knife he had last used to divide a pizza — but had never just casually chatted with them in a courtroom, never during their trial. 'Morning, Phil,' I'd say when I came into courtroom 11 to take my seat at the press bench directly behind this tiny figure dressed in a limited range of tiny dark suits and an unlimited range of crazily patterned socks; he'd respond with a wink and a cheerful word. Friends knew him as Polk or Polky. It was an appealing diminutive but I refrained from using it. 'See you tomorrow, Phil,' I'd say when I left, and he'd affectionately place his hand on my arm. In between times we gossiped, joked, laughed, made small talk, sometimes made big talk; he always stood up when I came over for a yarn, made that kind of gentleman's polite gesture. It was all very collegial, although many times I thought I ought to feel I was in the presence of evil.

Most murder-accused are marooned throughout their trial in the dock. It must feel like one of the loneliest places in the world, and yet one of the most public. It's a glass box, with a little waist-high door that leads to the downstairs cells. It's a room of accusation, a purgatory, a bad place to find yourself ordered to sit inside for everyone to stare at and judge.

Polkinghorne was not confined to this chamber of prejudice. He was landed gentry, owner of a block of real estate in the form of a row he had all to himself, behind his legal team in courtroom 11; the only times he appeared in the dock were at the beginning of the trial, to enter his plea, and at the very end, to hear the verdict. They were cameo appearances. Otherwise, he was part of the general courtroom population.

But it was more than just the geography that made him so accessible and allowed our tête-à-têtes. It was a class thing. Finally, after years of reporting on murder trials of damaged colonised peoples, or of low-lifes and the financially illiterate, I was able to relate to someone accused of depriving someone else of their life. 'Oh yes, I know who you are,' he said when I first introduced myself. He could read. He stood up, we shook hands, he said, 'Philip Polkinghorne.' It was all very formal, like men meeting at a function or a conference, and it was easy to assume a connection. We were men of a pension demographic — I was 64, he was 71 years old — and we shared the same cultural references as everyone in the white New Zealand middle class.

The point of my conversational ingratiations was to size him up. He was not of great size. One day when we were talking, I was trying to describe one of the witnesses: someone from his former eye clinic's executive team. I couldn't remember his name.

'Bit taller than you,' I said.

'Everyone's taller than me,' he said, and put on a hapless expression; he presented himself as Charlie Chaplin, little comical tramp.

The terrible thing about the trial was that it was so wildly entertaining. It ripped up the deep puritanical contract that New Zealanders signed up to when white settlers went about establishing the new colony. It liberated the country from shame. Polkinghorne was shameless. He was a sex machine in miniature. He maintained a furiously busy roster of sex workers, but it wasn't as though he wasn't getting it at home; in his only police interview, he casually revealed that he and his wife of 24 years had sex every day. The trial heard about group sex and professional orgies. A detective at the trial recited the synopses of the videos he watched on Polkinghorne's phone. 'She performed a sex act on him', etc. There was a balance sheet of Polkinghorne's sex spend, when a forensic accountant totted up the sums he gave to prostitutes. It echoed the self-service robot voice at supermarkets: *Do you wish to print a receipt?* The figure was wonderfully exact and certainly very generous: $296,646.23.

He could afford it. One year he charged $756,496.54 for his services as an eye doctor. Polkinghorne was not Rich List rich, but his lifestyle was splendidly representative of the loaded classes: the four-million-dollar home in Remuera; the five-bedroom summer house on the Coromandel; motoring across the Auckland Harbour Bridge in his white Merc with the licence plate RETINA and pulling up outside the North Shore apartment of his regular Friday-afternoon appointment with an alcoholic sex worker. He was so avid for it one Friday that he turned up fresh from the operating theatre in his surgical scrubs. God, he was busy, a restless, priapic soul with a personal trainer and an investment advisor. The trial served as a thrilling portrait of the dissipated rich. One of the great diseases of the age is Netflixia, a common neurological condition in which we gain pleasure from streaming true-crime psychosis, and for eight weeks, *Polkinghorne: The Trial* was something to binge on, to spectate, to make us wonder what went on in that home above a blue lagoon.

The core of the trial was a tragedy. Pauline Hanna was 63 when she died. Cause of death was compression of the neck. To the end of their days, her family will not accept that she died by suicide — but then neither did the jury, as expressed in the profoundly baffling note they gave to the judge on the final day of their deliberations. It was a note of two halves. It was like a riddle, and no one who heard or read it in court that morning could figure it out.

The first half read, 'Most of the people on the jury do not think there is enough evidence to support Pauline committing suicide.'

As a long, but I think useful, aside: the word 'committed' was used throughout the trial by both legal teams. I used it, once, in my early reporting, until I received an email from a reader:

> I used to use this wording, and never thought about the meaning or connotations of these two words together, until my brother died by suicide. Suffice to say, losing someone to suicide is devastating. One of the things it brings into sharp focus is the power of language. In this context, it's not commit, as in to make a commitment to something. It's commit in the context of a crime, as in to commit murder. Thankfully for surviving family members, suicide is no longer deemed a crime in this country. There's enough judgment, stigma, shame and blame around suicide as it is. I'm hoping you're able to convert it to appropriate wording in your writing.

Fair call. I am able.

Given that the jury did not hold with the defence position that Pauline had killed herself, the entirely rational expectation was that they agreed with the prosecution argument that she had been killed. But the second half of their note was a kind of nihilism. The jury did not believe in anything. It began with that dread word: 'However'. It's worse than a but; it's more confused than an if; it's a concept that has reversed the course of history. *I give you Eden. However, here's a snake.* 'However,' the note read, 'some people on the jury do not think that the Crown has supplied enough evidence that we can answer yes to the question, "Has the Crown made you sure that Dr Polkinghorne caused the death of his wife, Ms Pauline Hanna, by intentionally strangling her?" Please can we have some direction.'

So not suicide. But not murder, either. Were they even sure she was dead? I spoke with Pauline's brother, Bruce Hanna, right after that message was delivered. He was trying to decipher it. We agreed that the crucial word was 'some'. That could mean, we reasoned, maybe two jurors thought the Crown had failed to make them sure; perhaps the rest, the other nine, were satisfied the Crown had met the threshold.

But — no, wait; I mean, *however* — we were proven wrong. Maybe it was the other way around. Maybe only two jurors felt sure, or even just one. In his closing address, Polkinghorne's lawyer, Ron Mansfield, stood in front of the jury and asked them to consider the fact that his client had no sign of a defensive injury on the morning of Pauline's death. *No sign?* The police had made much of the fact that Polkinghorne had a small cut on his forehead. One juror responded to Mansfield's comment — how strange to open a kind of dialogue with a lawyer during his closing address — and angrily prodded her finger at her forehead. She was the one juror whom Mansfield thought he had lost.

The judge directed the jury to put aside the burden of proof regarding suicide and to turn their attentions entirely towards the burden of proof regarding murder. The prosecution case had lost its last hope. About 30 minutes after the verdict, the jury were led away by courtroom staff. Two of them held each other. They formed a tight group. They were like passengers taken off a shipwreck. But there was one person missing: the woman who had challenged Mansfield. She had left, by herself, about ten minutes earlier; it was as though she wanted no part of them anymore.

Earlier that same day, after my conversation with Bruce Hanna, I went back inside courtroom 11, that hothouse which served as home for eight intense weeks, to check on the jury's note. I remembered seeing that a word had been crossed out. I wanted to take a closer look to see which word.

The foreperson's handwriting was very nice, and his spelling was immaculate. The word crossed out was 'everyone'. It had originally read, 'Everyone on the jury do not think that the Crown has supplied enough evidence.'

It was a prophecy of their verdict. In the minds of Pauline's family, Pauline's friends, Pauline's colleagues, and at a rough guess something like 99.7 per cent of the nation, he had got away with murder.

---

All throughout the trial, neighbours and strangers kept coming up to me on the street — as a faithful diarist filing trial portraits each and every day in *The New Zealand Herald*, I had my old mug constantly on bylined display — and they all said they were absolutely sure Polkinghorne had killed his wife but that he would get away with it. For quite some time my own feelings on the matter were that he might not have killed his wife but that he would go down, even though the case against him was weak. So many contradictions, so much that was contrary; it was actually impossible to view the trial with any certainty, but I gave it my best shot right at the end, when Crown prosecutor Alysha McClintock gave her closing address. It was light on forensic detail, a weakness which resembled Polkinghorne's claim to innocence, but it made a strong case for common sense. It fashioned a persuasively terrifying Polkinghorne effigy out of bits and pieces of straw and told the jury to burn it. I duly reached for a box of matches. On the morning of the verdict, I wrote two different introductions intended for the *Herald*. This was in the style of ye olde standard journalism practice on election nights: for example, in 2005, I was assigned to write a story marking the historic win at the polls of incoming Prime Minister Don Brash. He lost. The story was thrown into the dustbin of history. So, too, was the version I wrote of the Polkinghorne jury reaching an alternative verdict:

> It ends. After all that, after everything, the murder trial of Dr Philip Polkinghorne has been ruled as just another foul and disgusting instance of domestic abuse, of violence towards women, of a husband killing his wife because he felt like it. Because his mind was likely blown by the death drug, methamphetamine. Because he thought he could get away with murder, and he so nearly did, at large and living large for sixteen months before he was arrested, and on trial for eight closely argued weeks which opened the door for reasonable doubt — but was finally closed when the jury foreman stood in courtroom 11 at the High Court of Auckland and said: 'Guilty.'
>
> The verdict ruled that Polkinghorne choked or strangled his wife Pauline Hanna to death on Easter Monday morning of 5 April 2021, and then had the high intellect and the low animal cunning to stage it to look like a suicide. Throughout the trial I characterised the Crown's portrait of Polky as

a malignant sex dwarf, an odious sex midget, an evil sex elf, a hateful sex goblin; they were all close to the truth. The verdict of the jury got closer. It confirmed him as a killer sex gimp.

New Zealand didn't exactly stop for the trial and there was a lot of legacy news media hype about it — gimp on trial, read all about it — but even a calm assessment would measure it as the trial of the century. It was the nine-week telling of a dissipated Auckland life, a cautionary tale of thinking you can do anything you choose, including murder.

The whole thing was fiction. The effigy fell to pieces. The case against him was rotten. 'A grave nonsense,' as Ron Mansfield put it, in his closing address, yelling at the jury in a fit of rage; at 2.21 p.m. on Monday 23 September 2024, the foreman stood in courtroom 11 at the High Court of Auckland and said of the murder charge: 'Not guilty.' There was an alternate charge of manslaughter. The foreman repeated: 'Not guilty.' The judge started thanking the jury but was interrupted by the registrar, who apologised that she had forgotten to ask the foreman if the verdicts were unanimous. He said yes, they were unanimous.

It was like an enormous zeppelin just collapsed, fell slowly to earth, landed with a wet, pathetic plop. The balloon did not burst. It wilted. The whole thing — trial of the century, black and steaming with the hot tar of scandal — was ruled as all for nothing, a parade of fantastic amounts of entirely insufficient evidence as gathered by a Z-team of detectives who succeeded in not just blackening the name of an eminent surgeon, but also completely trashing it for the pleasure of a spellbound nation.

Polkinghorne, tarred and feathered, hounded and mocked; Polkinghorne, whose name will live forever in the dark, festering basements of New Zealand murder trials, alongside other immortals such as Mark Lundy and David Bain, also Arthur Allan Thomas and Scott Watson, some or all of whom are likewise not guilty; Polkinghorne, who, up until the moment he tremblingly jabbed 111 on his landline at 8.11 a.m. on an Easter Monday in 2021, his fingers leaving blood on the number pads, was just another urban professional going about his business in a medical field that's even more polysyllabic than his name — ophthalmology — in which he excelled, brought the amazing grace of sight to the near-blind, and was the author or co-author of 78 publications ('Optic Nerve Head Haemorrhages Associated with Posterior Vitreous Detachment', etc.) with 22,999 reads and 1520 citations — but that Polkinghorne, that very real paragon of medical excellence, no longer exists. He has been well and truly cancelled.

I asked him one Friday afternoon during the trial about his weekend plans, and he said, 'I don't have a life anymore.' He has since picked up whatever pieces are left over of his existence and is enjoying the freedoms that many, many people would fervently rather were denied. But he will never be his old self. His murder trial depicted another Polkinghorne: the rutting dog of Remuera who spent that precise amount of $296,646.23 on hookers; the man who got busted with 37.7 grams of excellent methamphetamine and who had smoked it in a pipe emblazoned with the amusing name SWEET PUFF; who was accused of killing his wife so he could set up house with a massively reconstructed Sydney sex worker and her pack of chihuahuas; the little man who was littler than everyone but larger than life in his mad, exuberant, unchained socks, those emblems of his Dostoevskyan conviction that everything is permitted. He lived as he pleased. He created the legend of Polkinghorne.

CHAPTER 1

# The Pale and Dwarfish Dr Jekyll

The High Court of Auckland is a white-turreted castle in the most English corner of town. It's perched on the intersection of Waterloo Quadrant and Parliament Street, opposite the beautiful arboretum gardens surrounding Old Government House, where Elizabeth Windsor stayed the night in 1953 as the newly crowned Queen of England. Ideally located for the application of English law, it's a fort of justice, an old pile of bricks spooked by the cries of the dead. It constantly gives me the creeps, but I approached it with a spring in my step and a song in my heart on the opening day of the Polkinghorne trial on Monday 29 July 2024.

The news media were set to go gaga. I was eager to contribute some ga.

But I felt a bit abashed. I had only recently vowed to stay away from reporting court trials and made a big deal about it in the introduction of my book *The Survivors*, 'the final book in my trilogy of true-crime narratives', explaining:

> I come and go from the High Court of Auckland, and sometimes stay away for months; in the winter of 2023, though, I decided to report on three trials, back to back, two of them about the murder of children, lasting about seven weeks. I overdid it. I started to experience a kind of interference. A kind of static scrambled all the usual signals. I would look at the defendants, look at their families, wonder about their low-life experience, and think: *I am way out of my league. I don't get it. I have no idea who you are and what your lives are like.*

Polkinghorne, though, was different. I was nowhere near his earnings league, but we belonged to the same white mass of the New Zealand dream. We were both Kiwis made good from the boring Bay of Plenty — I grew up in Mount Maunganui, he went to Tauranga Boys' College. We had become members of the indoor proletariat. I looked at the defendant and felt no remove. Neither of us claimed any special intelligence. 'I was dropped on my head when I was born,' he casually remarked one day in court. I asked what he meant, and he said, 'Born stupid.' It was self-effacing and not to be taken entirely seriously, but he had a point and there was really nothing about him that could reasonably qualify — as the Crown put it, throughout its case against him — as a criminal mastermind.

When we spoke that first day, it was by accident: I was walking out of court looking at my phone and nearly tripped over him. The trial had not yet properly begun. He was sitting at the back of the court where the police usually sit and at first I thought he might be one of the detectives. The fact I didn't recognise him revealed the fact I hadn't actually taken much notice of his case before it came to trial. I knew some of the bare details, enough to realise his trial was set to become the biggest gift to legacy news media since Prime Minister Jacinda Ardern gave the industry $50 million during Covid, and I had seen the famous photo of him alongside his wife Pauline Hanna at a social event, but I wasn't looking at his face in that photo. No one really did. Everyone was staggered by his pants.

The photo was taken by Norrie Montgomery, that great modern chronicler of desperate Aucklanders at play. The occasion was the December 2018 launch of a new range of perfume. Inevitably, the venue was in Parnell. Mr and Mrs Polkinghorne stood together with tall glasses of gin with ice. She wore a fuchsia trouser suit, the jacket over her arm. He wore an alarming pair of red trousers with zips in the legs. They were Significant Pants, the Pants That Changed Everything — New Zealand turned its heart against him as soon as they saw him in these pants, which identified him as a libertine, a bondage warrior, enjoying every bit of his midlife crisis. The most devastating line in 'Daddy', Sylvia Plath's classic poem full of devastations, is when she declares, 'The villagers never liked you.' The villagers of New Zealand rose up against Polkinghorne and his kinky red pants and have never stopped shaking their pitchforks.

Yet in person, in court, away from the Significant Pants, Polkinghorne *still* had an extraordinariness about him. He had beautiful blue eyes and a mischievous smile. He looked a bit like — okay all bald men look alike, and all short bald men are replicants — Dave Dobbyn. He was tiny, a furry little mouse, but without any mousiness; he took his place in the world, he moved with confidence. Also, he found a way to look vivid. He wore lurid socks. He had a new pair every day: socks with pineapples, socks with crescent moons, socks with hoops, socks of every colour. A woman who appeared as a witness at the trial said in court, 'He's a man who likes to stand out.' The socks were like a protest. They were two little rebel flags. He had done nothing wrong; he could dress as he pleased, and it pleased him to dress vivaciously. His son, Taine, also wore mad socks in court, perhaps in tribute to his innocent dad. Taine also sported a motif of his father's life before his arrest: bow ties. Polkinghorne had worn a different bow tie every day of the week. They were a part of him, as essential as breathing. They were so ubiquitous that his amour, Madison Ashton, had to tell him on the eve of Pauline's service at Holy Trinity Cathedral in Parnell: 'Do not wear a fucking bow tie to the funeral.' She added, 'Keep the hat.'

News coverage of the funeral, held ten days after Pauline's death, was the last time I had read or seen anything about the case before it went to trial. I remembered that a lot of bubbles were released from the church when her casket was taken out to the hearse. There was no footage showing whether or not Polkinghorne had worn a fucking bow tie.

At that stage police were treating the death as 'unexplained'. The house was being held for forensic investigation. At the time of the funeral, Polkinghorne was essentially homeless. He went to stay with his sister, Ruth, and he was still there during his trial.

I mentioned to him one day that it didn't look as though he ever ironed his suit pants. 'I iron my shirts,' he said. 'First time I've had to iron anything in thirty years.' He put on a wistful expression, not exactly like Dave Dobbyn singing 'Whaling' but close.

There are worse deprivations than ironing — prison isn't the best experience — but it was a reminder of the exile he was banished to after police took approximately 0.01 seconds to regard Pauline's death as suspicious and sealed off the house. He was allowed back in to shower and pack a bag. A revelation in the documentary series which played after the trial was that an empty packet of methamphetamine was found on the bathroom floor. 'Not mine,' he told the programme. A Scene Visit was arranged during the trial; it had the classic appearance — vacuumed within an inch of its life, flowers stuffed in vases — of a house artfully arranged by interior decorators on behalf of a keen vendor. Going once, going twice, the home of New Zealand's most famous failed murder investigation, or as New Zealand Sotheby's International Realty put it:

> So private behind immaculately groomed hedges in manicured grounds, this magnificent 376 sq m home was superbly designed with a clever floor plan for unparalleled family comfort . . . Solidly built of masonry and weatherboard, detailed with copper spouting, the property embraces a beautiful leafy park-like setting . . . From the entry, the lounge with big shug [sic] windows opens through cavity sliders to the dining room . . . Last but not least, it has double internal garaging with a handy wine cellar at the bottom of the stairs.

A house is where you live, it's got all your stuff, it's where you wake up and go to sleep, it contains your existential soul in comfortable limbo — and Polkinghorne was evicted from all that, thrown out on the same day as Pauline's death. His lawyer, Ron Mansfield, spent quite a lot of time at the trial describing it as despicable. It wasn't a popular notion; it wasn't the version that took hold. Right from the start, and all throughout the trial, it was actually far more shocking to entertain the thought that Polkinghorne was wronged, that he woke up one morning to find his wife had hanged herself — and then instantly segued from one nightmare to the next, with the police holding him responsible. Yet the preferred version that swept the homes and offices of the nation was that Polkinghorne killed her and then had the means and the malice to stage a hoax of suicide. It was the narrative that corresponded with the devil in a pair of zipped-riddled pants.

---

One concern interrupted the song in my heart when I walked into the red-and-white candy box of the High Court for Day 1 of the trial, which was set down for six weeks but ended up heading into a ninth, with the verdict on Day 39. I was anxious that I wouldn't be able to get a seat on the press bench. That happened a few years ago at a murder trial and I got in a terrible sulk, forced as I was to sit in the public gallery with no special privileges as a witness to violent history. Polkinghorne's trial was doubtless going to be Full Press. I raced to get there early, hence the spring in my step.

Things worked out fine. I got my precious seat. The trial was Full Press, but Full Press isn't what it used to be: legacy news media took an absolute hiding in 2024, with redundancies and restructures galore, and an entire television network guillotined. There was only one TV camera in court. Footage was shared in a kind of news co-operative. The tattered, battered remains of the fourth estate did their best to cover the trial; a freelancer from *Metro* arrived three or four times, before moving to Otago; Radio New Zealand sometimes sent youths; there was a documentary maker, who talked to himself; *Stuff* was there, represented by the brilliant Catrin Owen, a fine-haired Welsh waif who liked to eat lunch in the deserted basement floor of the High Court; but only the *Herald* moved in like a ground force, occupying four seats, in responsible acknowledgement that some news stories in the public interest are especially interesting for their high weirdness and touch of evil.

From that first day, when the Crown and defence gave their opening addresses, setting out the synopsis of a narrative that kept the nation guessing for the next weeks about how it would end, the details were so immediately lurid, so allegedly diabolical, that it felt like a case from the golden age of tabloid journalism. It was as though the nineteenth century had come calling, inky, horrified and gothic.

The High Court elevator seemed to have come from that century, too. It was an old rust bucket that broke down on the morning of the first day. Disaster! We all had to climb one entire flight of stairs to courtroom 11 that opening fortnight, while machinists skilled in Victorian elevator pulleys were located. In the basement, meanwhile, 40 Kiwis were empanelled for the jury pool. Each of them had the number 11 pinned to their chest. They were brought up to the courtroom, having to huff and puff two entire flights of stairs, and were led in. The judge, Justice Graham Lang, gave notice it was a murder trial set down for six weeks. I have never seen so many potential jurors have a quick word with the judge to state their case for not wanting a bar of it.

Nine women and three men were approved. I have never seen a jury that behaved so impeccably, with such close attention. Their faces became familiar and so did their habits. The brains trust of the jury seemed to be an Indian woman in the front row who masterminded the paperwork. One day the defence produced documents and asked if the jury had seen them. Within seconds, that juror waved them in the air. The foreman was from England. An old wife's tale from criminal justice has it that the person who sits next to the elected fore is the one who really, really wanted the job. It's possible this described another woman with a proud moko kauae. She, too, sat next to the foreman and looked like she knew how to run the show.

The public gallery was filled. There was room for about 70. Their faces, too, would become familiar over the next eight weeks. Celebrity private investigator Julia Hartley-Moore turned up looking like a celebrity in a massive fur coat. She was there in her role as executive producer of documentary series, *Polk*, which screened after the trial. She appeared in her own documentary quite a lot to say almost nothing of interest, for example, a woman called her not long before Pauline died and said her husband was seeing prostitutes but then hung up, and it might have been Pauline Hanna who knows. At the back of the gallery, taking up four seats, was a team of detectives who worked on Operation Kian, the Polkinghorne case. They spoke to no one. Their officer in charge, a clerk with a weak chin, would not so much as say hello when leaving the court. The faint four formed a mute void.

Justice Lang — who began the trial with a rocker's wild hair, got it cut, and ended the trial six weeks later with his silver hair once again gone everywhere — was also a man of few words. There were very few challenges to the lawyers; his sessions in chambers were brief interludes of exchanged pleasantries; his closing address was over and done with in a morning. He presided over the trial with good grace, but I have never seen a judge so kindly disposed towards proceedings. Self-effacing, humble, calm, he was the judge who wasn't there.

Ron Mansfield KC was definitely there. His restless energy and high-strung nerves formed a kind of cone of tension around him in the courtroom. He was inevitably there; as the most famous defence lawyer in town, the big hitter, the gun for hire, of course he represented Polkinghorne. No one else was better suited. You wondered about the brilliant technique of David Jones KC, but his posh bearing was apt to send the wrong message of rich white privilege; Nick Chisnall KC is the smartest man in the room, but he was too pure of heart for a case so sordid. It had to be Mansfield, a street fighter with an awful honking nasal voice straight out of the Canterbury flatlands of his hometown, Waimate. He wore too-tight suits and an amusing cap on his shaved head. With pale eyes remote behind thick glasses, and little teeth that tore at the flesh of Gala apples every day in court, he could be marvellously witty company, but his chief characteristic was intensity. He was legendary for his work ethic. He put everything into it, long nights, weekends, all of that; the Polkinghorne trial would be his masterpiece.

He was up against the Big Two. Alysha McClintock served as the Crown solicitor; Brian Dickey held that role before her, left the Crown office in search of fresh challenges, but made a comeback, lured by the trial to end all trials. They made a formidable pair. McClintock buttoned herself up in her usual courtroom wardrobe of snug little Jackie Onassisian two-piece suits and went about her business with a seriousness of purpose. She had attended Wanganui Collegiate with another distinguished alumnus: Jeremy Wells, the broadcaster with his own specially created niche of cheerful, incessant mockery. He remembered her handwriting: 'Tall and weird like she's writing music,' he texted.

Dickey sloped into court like he'd just come in off a farm or fishing boat, chucked on a suit, and not had time to brush his hair. He wore an old raincoat. He sloped around the courtroom with his hands in his pockets. But there was something jarring about him one day in the opening week of the trial when he wore a new pair of black leather loafers with a buckle. It was the closest he has ever looked to resembling an Auckland wanker. Generally, he appeared throughout the trial as a good shambling Kiwi joker without a trace of pretension, but behind his relaxed demeanour was a firm and absolute commitment to prosecution.

I chatted with Dickey and McClintock during the trial, once or twice over a sandwich, and I always came away thinking they shared an animus towards Polkinghorne. It felt that this was not just another trial where they functioned as officers of the court. They both shared an actual genuine desire to make Polkinghorne pay for Pauline's death.

—

The very first thing Polkinghorne said in court was, 'Guilty.' It was at the start of the trial, when he was asked by the court registrar to answer a charge of possession of methamphetamine. She then asked him how he pleaded to a charge of possessing a pipe to smoke methamphetamine. Again, the quiet voice: 'Guilty.' With that out of the way, he faced a third charge, a kind of PS, just something for him to address, if he wouldn't mind: murder. 'Not guilty,' he replied. He never said another word in open court for eight weeks.

The methamphetamine charges were confusing admissions. What was an old rich guy doing with the drug of choice for the young and hopeless? Methamphetamine was the white ruin of provincial New Zealand, measured in the wastewater of towns with high unemployment; it was also the *best* drug on the market, as in the chemical product that gave the strongest, most exhilarating derangement of the senses, acting fast as a bolt of lightning and with just as much of an electric charge on the synapses. You smoked it; it smoked you; it was a column of flame, laying users to waste. The professional classes generally preferred happier drugs: ecstasy, cocaine, acid. Methamphetamine was hardcore, the last illicit drug in a permissive age. And yet here was the author of 'Optic Nerve Head Haemorrhages Associated with Posterior Vitreous Detachment' owning up to a stash, and a pipe to smoke the stash.

Polkinghorne left the dock and walked behind Mansfield to take his seat at the far end of a row. McClintock stood and gave her opening address. It was epic and lurid, packed with incident, a portrait of an evil so unique that it was stunning. She went straight to the death of Pauline Hanna, asserting that

Polkinghorne had killed her and staged it as suicide. There were injuries to her face, arms and back. There was a fresh injury on his forehead. Her bedroom was dishevelled. They were all clear signs of a struggle, she said.

And then she said:

> Dr Polkinghorne described his relationship with his wife as 'perfect', and 'quite good'. This marriage was far from perfect and quite good. It wasn't even plain old good. It had completely fallen apart. Dr Polkinghorne was living a double life, spending large amounts of money on sex workers. At the time of Pauline's death, he was in a long-term covert relationship with sex worker Madison Ashton. Pauline knew they had sex together and reluctantly accepted it and had joined them in threesomes in Australia. But she was becoming concerned with her husband's obsession with group sex and his demands that they have sex every day. She did not know he was seeing sex workers in Auckland and evidence will be brought to demonstrate this was a marriage in steep decline.

I have never seen an opening address illustrated with pictures. McClintock shared photos taken from the Polkinghorne home. It showed the lovely view of the golden pond of Ōrākei Basin. It showed a length of orange rope hanging from an upstairs balustrade. It showed Pauline's body beneath a duvet at the bottom of the stairs. 'Pauline was always immaculately dressed. But she wore nothing except a robe when she died, and was otherwise naked and dishevelled.' The rope, McClintock said, was too long and too loose to support a body.

She posited that on the night of 4 April 2021 things came to a head.

> He strangled her — either with his hands, a forearm or something soft and smooth around her neck. He did so, perhaps whilst angry and high or low, or just plain strung out on methamphetamine. Methamphetamine was found in various places in significant quantities. Maybe he lost it, and snapped, perhaps she rejected his sexual demands. We will never know. It sounds shocking, like something from a crime novel.

I could not think of a crime novel with such a relentlessly trashy narrative. But the worst of it was implied. Yes, worse than actual murder; the Crown case against Polkinghorne asked everyone to imagine what happened in their home after he killed her. The delicate term for it is post-death conduct. The post-death conduct, in the Crown scenario, pictured Polkinghorne, wired on methamphetamine, going to the incredible lengths of carrying his wife's body down the stairs, fussing around with a chair, a rope and a leather belt, and garrotting her to make it look like she had taken her own life. It was like a radio drama: listeners had to picture the tableau of it, the choreography of it. Polkinghorne creeping down the stairs with the weight and horror of his wife's dead body. Polkinghorne having the wit and the nastiness to find a length of rope and decide on using a belt; Polkinghorne dragging the chair from the dining room to the landing, and positioning her body on it, keeping it upright long enough to attach the belt to the rope. The toilet was unflushed and looked obscenely dark in police photographs taken the next day; there were traces of methamphetamine in the bowl. Were the curtains closed? Did he dim the lights? How long did it take? Was he crying, was there profound remorse for what he was doing, or even a thin peel of it? Or is this asking too much of him, of the character we were told by McClintock to imagine? Really all he was trying to do, as per the Crown's version, was get away with it. It was needs must. It was pragmatic. The thing was done; Pauline wasn't coming back; something had to be done about it. At what speed did the thought cross his mind, and at what speed was it executed? Was he careful, meticulous, a cool practitioner of a kind of scientific experiment? Certainly he had crossed over to the dark side. He was Dr Polkinghorne as Dr Jekyll, who 'began to go wrong, wrong in mind', as Robert Louis Stevenson puts it in his classic story, and who ended up as his monstrous Other:

> Mr Hyde was pale and dwarfish, he gave an impression of deformity without any nameable malformation, he had a displeasing smile, he had borne himself with a sort of murderous mixture of timidity and boldness, and he spoke with a husky, whispering and somewhat broken voice . . .

The awfulness of it was shooed away by Ron Mansfield. His opening address set out a prosaic version of events. 'There is nothing unexplained about her death. He simply went to bed and when he got up he found her dead.' Pauline was depressed. Pauline was on medication and drank heavily. The stress of her job on the Covid front lines was crushing. 'She struggled with mental health.' Her death was self-inflicted. 'Dr Polkinghorne simply went to bed and when he got up in the morning, he discovered his wife had hung herself.' Police found no evidence of an argument, no evidence of methamphetamine use, no evidence of any assault. As for the sex workers, 'Their lives were open and their sex life was open. Pauline was involved.' Police made up their minds it was murder within minutes and became obsessed with the desperate need to find evidence of a motive. 'A motive did not exist. But they upturned Dr Polkinghorne's life, this man who loved his wife, and she loved him.'

Murder, said the Crown; suicide, said defence; the chosen twelve of the jury were asked to separate fact from crime fiction.

CHAPTER 2

# Malignant Sex Dwarf

'He was,' Alysha McClintock said in her opening address, with severe and furious disapproval, 'a sex fiend.' What an incredible choice of words. I was really only paraphrasing when I composed my first portrait of the trial for the *Herald* that afternoon, and wrote, 'The Crown have signalled it will attempt to present Polkinghorne to the jury as a malignant sex dwarf.' It was the outraged sound of the nineteenth century, it was black swirling capes and smelling salts — it was starved and sooty-faced paperboys howling, 'Read all about it! Sex fiend! Or if you prefer, malignant sex dwarf!' It felt like it came from a time before Woke; this wasn't the contemporary code of #MeToo, it had no hashtaggable modernity, it arrived with the dark gothic appeal of something monstrous from a Victorian or Edwardian past.

And so the opening addresses were a box-office sensation. They led the news hours, were top of the bulletins; readership figures at the *Herald* were massive and remained so throughout the trial. George Block was the hardest-working man in the legacy news business, writing a witty, intelligent live blog for the *Herald* that was updated every fifteen minutes. Everyone looked up to him. He was 195 centimetres, or 6 feet 3 inches. Shy, observant, quietly manic, he fuelled his industry with the same packed lunch throughout nine weeks: peanut butter sandwiches with a smear of Marmite. Craig Kapitan, the newspaper's chief correspondent in the combat zones of court, wrote elegant, wonderfully concentrated summaries throughout each day. He was that rarest of contradictions, a quiet American, and looked like an old sea dog in his pointed beard and roll-neck jumpers of heavy thread. He sat next to the other most senior figure in Auckland court reporting, *Stuff* journalist Catrin Owen, who sometimes started the day at 5 a.m. to get to the gym for an hour-long workout at 6 a.m.; petite, blonde, shrewd, her first language was Welsh, but she had perfected the fluent language of trialese. None of them missed a day. I admired their professionalism and really valued their hearing. Being deaf as a post has its drawbacks in a room made entirely of spoken language. Otherwise, though, I was a picture of contentment. The trial was one of the most thrilling experiences of a lifetime — 44 years to be precise — in the journalism trade.

The windows of courtroom 11 faced east, in the direction of Polkinghorne's house. A plane tree took up the immediate view. It was bare and hard and smooth. It held up thin July light in its branches. The winter of 2024 felt like the coldest I had ever experienced in Auckland; no one seemed to feel it more than Polkinghorne, who sometimes wore a heavy overcoat in the opening weeks of the trial and complained about the coldness of the courtroom. The trial seemed to keep pace. It began slowly, with a wintery sense of caution. It created a sense of tension.

It conformed to the standard witness list in murder trials by calling the first responders. Ambulance staff described the scene at the Remuera house that Monday morning. There wasn't much to describe. Pauline's body lay beneath the duvet. Her head was on a stair. A pillow had been placed beneath it. A cut length of orange rope dangled from the balustrade. Polkinghorne wore a dressing gown. Responders were asked quite a lot of questions about his demeanour. They described him as 'composed' and 'calm'.

New Zealand never forgave Mark Lundy for breaking down in loud hysterics at the funeral of his wife and child. He was overdoing it, said the public; it revealed that he was, in fact, their killer. He was acting. He was too emotional. Yet now Polkinghorne was being held up for not being emotional enough. He was cold. He was weird. His manner revealed, Crown prosecutor Brian Dickey suggested with his repeated questions, that he was his wife's killer.

I don't know if it added up to anything. At lunch on the second day of the trial, I disappeared into one of the giant leather armchairs at nearby Old Government House and read the latest *London Review of Books*. It featured a review of a book about Emily Dickinson and quoted from one of her poems: 'After great pain, a formal feeling comes.' I thought about that back in court as Dickey continued to pose questions about Polkinghorne's demeanour. It seemed to me that Dickinson was meaning the way we sometimes respond to a crisis, a tragedy, a loss that may be a death, or, just as devastatingly, feel like death, by going about our business in an orderly manner. Something has come undone. Nothing can fix it. All that we can face is to make a cup of tea, answer the phone, observe whatever other formalities. Life goes on. Best not keep the funeral director waiting.

Constable Alexander Rowland appeared as a witness. He spoke with Polkinghorne on the morning of Pauline's death. Polkinghorne asked him, 'Do you mind if I make a cup of tea?'

The officer said that was alright.

Polkinghorne asked, 'Would you like one, too?'

The officer said no thanks.

Polkinghorne returned from the kitchen with two cups of tea. Politeness is often the first thing to go in a crisis, but there was Polkinghorne fetching the unwanted tea for his guest, squeezing the teabag against the cup, observing the formalities . . . I was fancying that I saw the ghost of Emily Dickinson moving among the teacups, absolving Polkinghorne of any weirdness.

I visualised, too, the futility of that unwanted cup of tea. Yet the very nature of so much of the Crown case was an exercise in uselessness. It had nowhere else to go except travel in the empty territories of uselessness. It occupied uselessness. These geographies are all synonyms for that dread state known as circumstantial evidence. In essence everything they came up with was no more substantial than the very first sign of doubt that Pauline had taken her own life. Constable Alexander Rowland, he who was made a cup of tea that he didn't want, explained in the witness box on Day 2 of the trial that a sergeant at the scene had turned to him at one point and scribbled '1-C' on the palm of his hand. It was police code for 'suspicious circumstances'. All of it, the sixteen months of Operation Kian, the nine weeks of the prosecution's side in court, could be reduced to a single number and a single letter. The whole case, in fact, was just 1-C vs Polkinghorne; the volumes of the Crown's detailed paperwork only as pertinent as an inked hieroglyphic on an open palm. You could say its science was based on palm reading.

The 1-C evidence promptly got smudged. To Brian Dickey, Rowland said he read his sergeant's palm after he took a statement from Polkinghorne, at 10.45 a.m.; to Mansfield, though, he admitted that he read the sergeant's hand an hour earlier. Polkinghorne dialled 111 at 8.11 a.m. First responders arrived at 8.24 a.m. (Polkinghorne's sister Ruth arrived in between.) Police arrived at 8.55 a.m. The 1-C message was presented at 9.45 a.m. It took less than an hour to get the first documentary evidence that led to a homicide investigation; from there, the police never really seemed to stray from that position, although officers claimed in cross-examination they kept 'an open mind'. As in, I think, they were open to nailing Polkinghorne for the death of his wife.

---

The thing that started everything, that inspired the self-graffitied 1-C, was when a detective walked up the stairs of the Polkinghorne home to inspect the orange nylon rope that was tied around the balustrade and performed the so-called 'tension test'. The tension test was the foundation myth of the Polkinghorne case. It was performed by Sergeant Christian Iogha.

There were actually two little rope experiments. Iogha said in the witness box that the knot had not been pulled to the base of the banister. He found it odd; he expected the weight of Pauline's body to have pulled the knot back. He described putting his finger on top of the knot and gently pushing down to see if it would budge. It did, he said, moving about a centimetre or so with minimal pressure applied. 'Our purpose was just to see if the rope would stay where it was if there was pressure on it,' he said. 'At that point, I didn't believe it would sustain any weight.'

He then described giving the rope a yank: this was the tension test.

It was performed alongside Detective Ilona Walton, who later that day played a crucial role in the Polkinghorne investigation. Iogha, she said in the witness box, gave the rope 'a gentle, light pull' using his finger and thumb. 'It very quickly unravelled. It just kept going and going and going and going — extending out from where he was holding it. It seemed unusual and not normal that the rope would unravel in that manner.'

The unravelled rope, 'going and going and going and going', falling down the stairwell, into a void — the whole of the Polkinghorne inquiry was like that. The Crown held up the rope with disgust, as if between finger and thumb, just as Iogha had. This rope, they said, did not kill Pauline Hanna. They let it fall. 'It was too loose,' as McClintock said in her opening address, 'and too long.'

The rope evidence elevated the tension in courtroom 11. Polkinghorne's hoax was exposed. It seemed that he really had tried to stage a suicide, but botched it, making a bad job of tying the knots. And so the jury and everyone else were once again being asked to imagine the whole ghastly spectacle of the little ophthalmologist creeping around his house, maybe in the middle of the night, or in the darkest hours before dawn, intent on lynching his dead wife.

Except, as the defence argued, the rope evidence, the tension test, was based on a false premise. Polkinghorne had been instructed by the 111 operator to cut the rope. He had also, as he told police that day, undone the knot — because the sight of the rope was 'hideous'. The tension test was moot. Of course it was loose. He had loosened it.

When the Crown produced a copy of its witness list at the start of the trial, it had been exciting to note that the fifteenth witness was a Dr Robert Chisnall, described as 'a forensic rope analyst'. A forensic rope analyst! An expert in that arcane field would surely reveal the truth about Polkinghorne's critical mistake with the rope. Chisnall duly appeared on the Thursday of the opening week. His long old face filled the screen; he was coming in by video link from his home in Ontario. It was as though he'd never placed a Zoom call before, and figured the best way to go about it was to stick his face as close as possible to the camera. It made him look terrifying. It made him look like novelist William Burroughs, thin-lipped and severe, a prophet of doom. He duly described performing tension tests with a rope in the same configuration as the one in the Polkinghorne case: 'Multiple times I pulled on the rope. Very little force was required to cause it to collapse. The results were the same all the time . . . It was too long and too insecure to suspend any weight.'

Devastating, until cross-examination. The first question Mansfield asked Dr Chisnall was whether he was actually a doctor.

He said he wasn't. He conceded he did not have an engineering degree, instead holding a Master of Arts degree in education and a BSc, and held no academic position related to ropes, or knots, or forensics, but he added he had authored many papers on the subject of ropes, and quite liked rock climbing. 'Thank you,' said Mansfield, 'Mr Chisnall.'

Mr Chisnall's experiments were performed on the back porch of his house. Perhaps laboratories are scarce in Kingston, Ontario. No, he said, he did not use the actual rope or the actual balustrade from the Polkinghorne case. Mansfield showed him photos of Institute of Environmental Science and Research (ESR) staff removing the balustrade and rope, and wrapping them in cardboard for forensic examination. He asked Mr Chisnall if they were sent to his home. He said they were not.

Mansfield then informed him that the same kind of rope could be bought from Supercheap Auto, and asked one of the great questions in the history of New Zealand criminal cross-examination: 'Have you heard of Supercheap Auto?'

Mr Chisnall said he had not.

Mansfield informed him the same kind of rope could also be bought on eBay. Yes, said Mr Chisnall, he had heard of eBay, but no offer was made to send him the rope on eBay or from the hallowed premises of Supercheap Auto. He made do with whatever ropes he had lying around at his house in Kingston, Ontario. 'They would behave in the same way,' explained Mr Chisnall. Mansfield also asked him about the fundamental misconception about the rope: i.e., that it was loose because Polkinghorne had loosened it. Mr Chisnall agreed the shape of the rope indicated it could have been partially untied.

The long old face loomed on the screen. When he was giving evidence in chief to the prosecution, his similarity to William Burroughs was a stern reminder of the great novelist's famous remark about murder: 'Nobody owns life, but anyone who can pick up a frying pan owns death.' The admonishment in his face made you think of Polkinghorne picking up a rope and a belt and owning death by disowning himself of any responsibility. By the end of his cross-examination, though, the only connection to be made between Mr Chisnall and William Burroughs was the reminder that so much of Burroughs' fiction reads so poorly, so nonsensically, so speculatively, so unconvincingly.

---

Defence do not share a witness list in trials. They hold it close, keep it a secret; and what everyone wanted to know in the Polkinghorne trial was whether the defendant himself would be called to give evidence, to account for his movements, to sing his song of innocence. The mystery lay there, still and reptilian, as the trial progressed. This, too, was another tension felt in courtroom 11.

While we waited, we did actually hear from Polkinghorne in the opening fortnight, three times: each time revealingly, each time full of clues, signs, hidden meanings.

There was the 111 call.

'What is your emergency?' the operator asked.

'My wife's dead,' said Polkinghorne. 'She's hung herself.' His voice was panicked, traumatised; he was crying, and breathing hard. He gave his name and address.

'She's hung herself, is that correct?'

'Yes. Yes,' he sobbed.

'Cut her down immediately.'

'Cut her down,' he repeated. 'Cut her down. Yeah.'

'Can you cut her down?'

'Yep.'

He dropped the phone. You could hear him grunting in the distance. Only much later, when Alysha McClintock gave her closing address, were we asked to remember the time that passed between him getting off the phone and getting back on it. That gap, she said, was an important clue. The 111 call was like a radio drama: all you could go on was sound, and the spaces in between the dialogue.

Polkinghorne returned to the phone. He asked, 'You there?'

The operator confirmed she was there. She said an ambulance would get there soon. Polkinghorne's breathing was very sharp. His voice broke. He whimpered. The operator asked, 'Why do you believe that she's dead?'

He said, 'I can't feel a pulse. I'm a doctor. She's blue. She's cold.'

'Is she awake?'

'No,' he replied. 'No!'

That last exchange, at least, was definitely accurate. Pauline was 100 per cent not awake. By the time responders arrived, her body was laid on the floor and covered with a duvet. She was wearing a gown pulled down around her waist. She had no underwear on beneath the gown. Her head was tilted to the left and there were obvious markings on her neck, about 3 centimetres in width with a criss-cross-type pattern, like diamond shapes. There appeared to be a reasonably fresh cut to the left side on the bridge of her nose.

There was blood coming out of her left ear, some bruising on her inner right thigh and blood between her fingers. Police photos of her body showed a hand had come free beneath the bedding. The top of her dark hair was showing. Next to her were three full bowls of cat food.

Police arrived after St John's medical officers. Polkinghorne was asked to give a statement. It was rendered in the kind of formal language that only exists in police statements. He told a banal story, which is to say he described the typical New Zealand evening. They had dinner on the night of 4 April. They drank wine in 'the library' (the house had four bedrooms and four bathrooms). On the last night of her life, Pauline watched two episodes of medical drama *New Amsterdam* on Netflix. She went to bed at about 10 p.m. Polkinghorne put on the dishwasher. Police found a wine glass on the counter the next morning, smeared with Pauline's lipstick. The couple slept in separate bedrooms that night. Lights out in Ōrākei, the tide creeping towards and away from the lovely oval basin; another peaceful Easter in the pretty eastern suburbs of Auckland.

Polkinghorne got out of bed at about 7.40 a.m. on 5 April and put on a dressing gown over his pyjamas. He walked downstairs to make tea and toast, and at this exact point his story departs from the standard New Zealand drudgery because he walked through to the other side of the house and saw Pauline's body slumped forward on a chair, with a belt around her neck, looped to an orange rope from a balustrade at the top of the stairs. He called 111.

He said in his sworn statement:

> I was very flustered. I knew she was deceased. I tried to call 111 on my cellphone but I was so flustered I couldn't get it to work. I used my landline in the kitchen to call 111.
>
> Once that call was ended, I undid the belt and rope from around Pauline's neck and then went upstairs to undo the knot from the cord. I'm not sure at what point I've done this but I rolled up the belt that was around Pauline's neck and put it in the kitchen.
>
> Pauline has been on and off depressed for several years. She takes some antidepressant medication. I'm not sure what it's called. She has been taking it for several years. I'm not sure if she still has been taking it recently. She also has suffered from bulimia about five years ago. She has been taking weight reduction medication also. Pauline has been exhausted in recent times. This has been mainly from working such long hours.

While Polkinghorne was giving this sworn statement — outside, on the patio — detectives were inside the house, whispering among themselves. There were red flags everywhere they looked, alarm bells clanging in their heads. There was the tension test. There were the injuries to Pauline. There was the fresh cut on Polkinghorne's forehead. There was the bizarre disarray of Pauline's bedroom: an ottoman tipped on its side, pillows on the floor, the top sheet missing, a dark stain on the bottom sheet. There was, above all, the strangeness of Polkinghorne himself, that obviously wealthy sprite who struck one observer at the scene as remarkably unconcerned when he casually walked past his wife's body to climb the stairs and change out of his dressing gown. Detective Walton had asked him if he would accompany her to the police station to provide 'just a few more details'. She said, 'He happily obliged.' They set off for the new station in College Hill, Ponsonby, and stopped at a petrol station to get Polkinghorne a muffin. He only ate half of it and left the other half on the little table between himself and Walton in the little room where he talked, and talked and talked and talked, for three hours and 58 minutes.

He raved. He gabbled. He monologued. Some detectives maintain a cold silence, to provoke their suspect into filling the silence with incriminating yap. Walton didn't need to manipulate Polkinghorne to open his mouth. He seldom shut his mouth. She could barely get a word in edgeways. He jumped up at one point to mimic how he found Pauline's body slumped forward on a chair — 'You don't have to do this,' Walton said, but he didn't listen.

The video was shown in court on a video screen. A transcript was provided to the jury. They could watch Polkinghorne, in pink shirt and jeans with a jaunty sunhat on the table. Yappy, wanting to express every little thing, at ease with his physical presence in the little room, he settled himself on the two-seater couch and spread his legs. They could take their eyes off him and read Polkinghorne's ravings. But what sense could they make of anything? What the hell was it all about? Who talks like that, in the hours after their wife has hanged herself? All Walton had to say, over and over, dully, in response to the many and varied little boastings, was, 'Wow.'

He mentioned the spacious wardrobe in his house: 'Some might say excessive!' He mentioned the ensuite 'master' bedroom: 'Sounds a bit sexist!' He mentioned his love of French Earl Grey tea: 'Isn't it fantastic!' He mentioned doing the housework: 'I'm not a saint, don't get me wrong. I'm not going around polishing the floors.' He mentioned the dinner she cooked on her last night: 'I say it's the best I've eaten all year and stuff like that.' He mentioned what she drank that night: 'She poured Pinot into the Shiraz glass because she was less interested about the palate, shall we say.' So much of what he said sounded . . . inappropriate. The nadir was when Walton asked him when he and Pauline last had sex. 'I think Saturday,' he said. 'Or yesterday? We were intimate just about every day.'

The jury rolled their eyes, sighed, laughed out loud in disbelief as he continued to free-range any subject that came to his mind: mosquitoes, showers, their summer house, toast, pillows, dogs. But he also addressed Pauline's death.

He said he came downstairs and put the toast onto a low setting. It was habit to put it back in to brown it after the tea was made. But the bread was never browned:

> For some reason I walked down to the other end of the house, and I saw Pauline and she was slouched on a chair. Her dressing gown was half on and half off. Her arms were blue. She was cold. Her face was contorted. She was very blotchy. I could tell she was dead straight away.
>
> I tried to put her down flat. I think they told me to do that. It was just like having an arm pulled off you. It was horrible. When I got her off the chair, the dressing gown was all over the place. Her legs buckled and it was a dog's breakfast.
>
> I'm just trying to think, why was she sitting there in the chair? Maybe she was standing on a chair and went off and . . . maybe, I don't know.

Mainly he sat in the corner of his two-seater couch. Now and then he moved closer to Walton; the terrible thought occurred that he was on the pull, getting intimate, flirting. Sometimes she took a break and left him in the room alone. The hours passed; the interview dragged on. When she signalled that they were about to take another break, he asked, 'Can I go for a walk then?'

She said, 'Probably not.'

She left the room. He was standing up when she returned. He said, 'Is it cold or is it just me? I'm shivering.'

And then it was back to all the mentions, the by-the-ways, the madly boring small talk in the hours after he had lost his wife. He mentioned that she slept with the windows and even the doors open: 'It was like having a howling gale.' He mentioned she liked to turn on the shower, then leave, close the door, and only return when it was filled with steam: 'In the meantime she'd go off and milk the cows or something, I don't know.' He also mentioned they had argued about staining the deck of their summer house: 'I'm trying to find out a whole lot of things that may have triggered it,' he said, as though staining a deck might drive someone to suicide.

It finally ended. I thought: *That was the worst interview I've ever seen anyone give to the police*. I thought: *The guy seemed out of his mind, jumpy, manic, weird, untrustworthy, wildly inappropriate, desperate to make chit-chat about showers, mosquitoes, toast — he just wasn't acting right*. I thought: *There is no way Mansfield will agree to this raving lunatic appearing as a witness in his own defence*. I looked over at Polkinghorne in court, small and glowering in his dark suit and his mad socks and thought: *You are surely 100 per cent guilty*.

CHAPTER 3

# The Midnight Clock

Every morning, I walked to court through the lovely grounds of the University of Auckland campus. Every morning of the four-week Crown case, the hands of the university's filigreed clock tower were stuck at 12. It felt like an accurate commentary. Showdown at high noon, or the chimes of midnight — either time was right, as the Crown's black-clad accusers Brian Dickey and Alysha McClintock directed the slow, steady journey through the wastelands of a death in Remuera.

Much of a Crown case is rote. It's customary for a prosecutor to recommend to the jury that they regard pieces of evidence as strands in a rope, each fibre twisting together and strengthening it, but the image was best avoided in the Polkinghorne trial for obvious reasons of taste; Dickey and McClintock went the other standard way and recommended to the jury that they regard evidence as pieces of a jigsaw. Each shape would interlock to form the picture that most resembled guilt. Piece by piece, the jigsaw came into view at courtroom 11; the prosecutors started at the corners and formed a frame; the process was patient, meticulous, assured.

Yet on Tuesday 13 August, three weeks into the trial, they presented a piece that shattered the university clock with its fixed hands, altered the time-space continuum to its correct axis, and I noted down the exact moment of a statement so incredible that it felt like the tolling of an ominous bell. It was heard at 10.51 a.m. It was met with complete silence, a silence of horror and terrible realisation. It silenced the press bench. It even silenced the public gallery, which earlier had been standing room only — until those who were standing by the door spotted a few seats at the far end, and a bunch of first-year louts from the University of Auckland law school duly headed that way, making a ruckus as they stomped on the feet of Pauline Hanna's family to get to their precious destination. Stomped and stomper were silent alike when the statement was made by the Crown's thirty-seventh witness whose appearance in court was as inevitable as Ron Mansfield's: Dr Kilak Kesha, the Crown pathologist based at Auckland City Hospital.

I have seen Kesha many times in murder trials. He sets out the maps of human suffering. The last time I had seen him was giving evidence of a fatal stabbing: 'The wound path was through the soft tissues of the front of the left shoulder and left chest, through the second left rib, entered the left side of the chest cavity, into the left lung and injured a major vessel in the left lung.' Fat-faced, phlegmatic, unsmiling, his hair long at the back and short in the front in a kind of lazy mullet, he has never seemed entirely comfortable in a courtroom. His appearance at the Polkinghorne trial was to prove the least comfortable of his life.

He began by telling the jury he has performed about 4000 autopsies. He has trained on the dead in Connecticut, Baltimore and Detroit. 'I systematically dissect every organ,' he said. I wondered whether Dr Kesha knew Dr Polkinghorne, who told police about going to the hospital morgue to collect eyes from donors. 'Yeah course,' Polkinghorne said when I asked. The two doctors sat in courtroom 11 and studied an exhibit book of photographs taken at Pauline's autopsy. Neither showed any emotion. Doctors have seen everything. But this was Polkinghorne's wife. I caught a glimpse of the booklet one day: there was a colour photo of Pauline's bare back, with small bruises on it.

The pathologist told the jury that Pauline had an abrasion on the bridge of her nose, and a cluster of bruises on the back of her right arm. She also had small pinpoint haemorrhages on her neck, sometimes visible in people who have epileptic fits, episodes of violent coughing, and hiccups, but most commonly from obstruction of the veins in the neck. He went on to say a bruise on her scalp meant that either something hit her head, or her head hit something. And then the subject turned to the impression the belt had made on Pauline's neck. That is: *what* impression? He said there was no impression made by the belt when he examined her body the day after her death and when Dickey asked what that suggested to him, I looked at the courtroom clock and wrote down the time of 10.51 a.m. to record the exact moment he replied,

'It suggests to me that most likely the belt was placed on the neck after death.'

And there it was, out in the open, confirmation of the monstrous and unequivocal shape of Polkinghorne skulking around his house and tying a belt around his dead wife's neck, remorselessly and intelligently acting out his gross charade of suicide, so determined to get away with killing her that he fell to the lowest registers of human psychopathy by engaging in the indelicate insults and indignities of post-death conduct. He deprived Pauline of her life, and now he deprived her of the truth.

In the silent courtroom, high noon and midnight converged on the stroke of 10.51 a.m. Morning tea was called at 11.30 a.m. I took my thermos of instant coffee and took my usual seat outside the court, a little nook which I shared with my *Herald* colleagues George Block and Carolyne Meng-Yee. Caro knew more about the case than anyone, including the police. She had scooped the only interview Polkinghorne had given, when she called him a few days after Pauline's death and he came up with his mangled remark that he was being treated by the cops as 'a person of suspect'. We sat together at the morning break and excitedly whispered to each other about what we had just heard. It was all over. There was no coming back from that. Polkinghorne had done it and his foul little antics had been found out.

Where to, then, for Ron Mansfield? Pathology reports defeat the best defence lawyers in murder trials. Mansfield was the best, but surely there was nothing he could do to minimise Kesha's stunning revelation.

Mansfield was generally scornful of the Crown's jigsaw. He regarded it as a grotesque caricature. His task was to scatter the pieces, tear at their edges and reduce them to soft, misshapen pulp, just the way his sharp little teeth tore at his beloved Gala apples each day in courtroom 11. And so it was that he stood to cross-examine Dr Kesha and perform an autopsy on a living person.

Things began in a collegial manner. 'You say the impression on the neck is inconsistent with a hanging,' said Mansfield. 'Shall we just explore that?' It wasn't as though Dr Kesha had a choice. For the next hour he experienced an onslaught. Mansfield was in the form of his life at the Polkinghorne trial and provided a cross-examination masterclass — a shame the law-school oafs had already hoofed it, marching out during morning tea. I was accosted by their law professor a few days later at Old Government House. I had described his students as 'louts' in the *Herald* and they were very upset about it, he said; one of them felt 'triggered'.

Back to the live autopsy. Mansfield raised the subject of Dr Kesha attending the police investigation at the Polkinghorne residence on the morning of Pauline's death, and asked, 'You saw what was clearly a belt impression on her neck, didn't you?'

'Yes.'

'Consistent with Pauline taking her life by her own hand?'

'Correct. It's a possibility.'

'If the belt was removed one or two hours after her death, that might explain why the impression was there on the fifth [of April] and not the sixth?'

'It's possible.'

He reminded Kesha that Polkinghorne told 111 that he removed the belt and cut the rope. And with that, the phantom of Polkinghorne, summoned by the Crown to perform dastardly deeds in the darkness of his home, promptly disappeared; the spell was broken; the jigsaw was a total mess. The belt, Kesha conceded, was very possibly placed on the neck *before* death.

Mansfield ramped up the cross-examination even more. The usually unflappable Kesha very often replied very flappably. Mansfield pressed him on why it seemed that his evidence in court was the first time he said the position of the belt's impression — horizontal, rather than upwards that would be consistent with a hanging — might have some significance. 'I told police on day one!' he shouted.

But there was nothing in his original report. 'Why not?'

Kesha: 'I wasn't asked.'

Mansfield sighed and said: 'It's not a matter of being asked! You're an expert in this area. If this was of significance, why didn't you refer to it?'

Kesha: 'Well, I didn't refer to toxicology, and I thought that was relevant, too!'

There were more angry exchanges, shouts, scorns. Things eventually calmed down. Mansfield asked, almost gently, 'Does your overall conclusion remain that suicide by hanging is a plausible explanation?'

Dr Kesha: 'That's correct.'

The storm had passed. The final hour of cross-examination saw Mansfield and Kesha sail together across an ocean of agreeableness. Yes, Kesha agreed, there was nothing on Pauline's body that indicated it had been dragged downstairs. Yes, Kesha agreed, she had no injuries indicating she was punched or kicked or forced into a wall. Yes, Kesha agreed, there were no injuries you might expect to see in a manual strangling.

Mansfield handed him back to Brian Dickey for re-examination. There wasn't much Dickey could do. As for Kesha: he started raving about percentages of genetic forms in the population, and suddenly turned his attention to Alysha McClintock — sitting quietly in court, not having any direct involvement with the Crown witness, just minding her own business — and asked her, 'What colour are your eyes?'

'Uh — hazel,' she replied, doing her best not to look bewildered but losing the fight.

And so a good day, in the end, for Polkinghorne. He had spent much of the day looking at photos of his wife's dead body in the post-mortem booklet. As the afternoon wore on, he closed the booklet and sat with his elbows on the table and his head in his hands. Were they images of a woman who had been murdered or who had died by suicide? Either way, he could look no more.

---

Throughout the trial I entered into a text correspondence with a criminal defence lawyer whom I had met in Wellington. His insights into the Polkinghorne trial were like an inside track. He was almost in awe of Ron Mansfield. At the start of the second week, I texted him, 'Ron's actually really quite good, isn't he.' He replied, 'He's superb. I think he's very clever, and trial fit.' Trial fit! It was a revealing way of putting things. He explained, 'As in, doing trials all the time and completely comfortable with the process.' But I saw it in a different way, specific to the Polkinghorne trial. It was a massive challenge. It surely at least sometimes must have felt overwhelming; even with Mansfield's track record, this marked the zenith of his career, the trial he will be remembered for, his legacy. And so it was a test of nerve, of endurance, of stamina, of resources, of mental strength, along with the usual alienated position held by all criminal defence lawyers as the second-most-hated person in the courtroom. Mansfield stayed fit. He remained vigilant, alert. He also remained on edge. He was nervous as a cat on the opening day of the trial and seldom relaxed. His daily diet adhered to Wittgenstein's philosophy on sustenance: 'I don't care what I eat so long as it is always the same.' As well as the Royal Gala apples, Mansfield also drank a vile green protein drink every morning in court, and every afternoon he gobbled almonds he brought along in large, noisy brown paper bags. They were like superstitions, like amulets or crosses or beads to cling to and to offer protection — to keep him in a state of grace, to keep him fit.

It worked. It was Mansfield's trial. 'It feels cobbled together,' my legal correspondent remarked of the prosecution case, and I had the feeling that it never really got started, never really had lift-off. It was as though they were forever serving meals on chipped plates, with cutlery that hadn't been washed. Mansfield was able to scorn Kesha's attempted big reveal about the lack of belt impressions on Pauline's neck and hurl the paltry scraps into the trash. Mansfield was able to scorn the evidence about the 'tension test' of the rope, and hurl that into the trash, too. When he asked police officer Christian Iogha whether he had filmed or photographed the test and found that no, Iogha hadn't, Mansfield rebuked him for failing to do so. Iogha replied, 'In hindsight, recording it would have been a good option.'

With one last crash, another meal was sent back, the plate cracked and now smashed as it, too, was hurled into the bin.

Mansfield's predecessor as the number 1 defence lawyer in town, Barry Hart, who ruled the High Court of Auckland in his 1990s and 2000s pomp, was at his most effective in cross-examining police. His openings and closings were crass and charmless. But some inner rage was let loose in cross-examination, and every cop who ever felt the brunt of his attack learned to hate Hart. My experience in courtrooms has led me to think they hate Mansfield, too. I felt that they particularly hated him at the Polkinghorne trial. Other witnesses felt the same. There was nothing unusual in that. It's not so much an occupational hazard in criminal defence as an occupational necessity. The crucial difference, though, between Hart and Mansfield is that the cops seemed to *fear* Mansfield.

Iogha got a rough ride in the many hours of his cross-examination. He was made officer in charge of the scene on 6 April, the day after Hanna's death, and remained in situ for the next week; in a sense, the buck stopped with him.

Yes, he told Mansfield, police and ESR staff spent long hours examining the property.

'Can we agree,' asked Mansfield, 'that the New Zealand police were looking for any evidence of a struggle or an assault at the house?'

Iogha could not agree. He said police were keeping an open mind to any evidence that might have disproved a struggle or an assault. Mansfield could not agree with that. Iogha, he said, did not have an open mind and was adamant the death was suspicious from the moment he conducted his tension test on the orange rope.

But from there, just like Kesha the pathologist, Iogha entered into a season of agreement. Yes, he agreed with Mansfield, if Pauline had been killed in a struggle in the bedroom, she would have needed to be dragged down the stairs to the landing.

'And as I understand it from the very careful examination of this room,' Mansfield asked, 'there were no indications other than what you have told us of any blood being identified in that room either by way of a visual examination or a luminol testing that was considered to be relevant?'

Iogha agreed.

Mansfield then said that as he understood it, there were no indications of Pauline having been dragged across the carpet.

Iogha agreed.

Speaking further on the lack of evidence for how Pauline might have been moved from the bedroom, Mansfield remarked there were no forensics to tell us how that might have occurred.

'Yes that's correct,' Iogha agreed.

Mansfield's theme was that it was a rush to judgment, and that an extraordinarily long time was spent on examining the house with very few tangible results. What did the cops have to show for it? What evidence did they find of a struggle, of a body being dragged to the downstairs landing, of murder? When Polkinghorne returned home after his gruelling police interview on the day of Pauline's death, he was allowed to take a shower and grab some clothes and he was sent packing. He was told, 'Police have changed their reasoning for being at the scene.' He was exiled to stay with his sister. Armourguard security patrolled his house. Eight days went by, including the day of Pauline's funeral.

'You put in some long hours,' Mansfield said to Iogha.

'It's longer than normal.'

Mansfield stared at him. He asked, 'The longest?'

'For me personally? Correct.'

But even then, he valiantly tried to sidestep that it had broken the record for a scene examination and tried to maintain the delusion that it was standard procedure. Mansfield said to him, 'New Zealand police had this place searched and examined, not just for a long time. It's practically unprecedented.'

Iogha kept a stiff upper lip. He said, 'You can say that, but it's a big house.'

He was followed in the witness box by crime scene scientist Fiona Matheson, who was from the ESR. She told the court she found blood on the buttons of Polkinghorne's phone, on door handles, and a tiny bloodstain crossing two tiles across the grouting in Pauline's ensuite bathroom, but during the seven long days of her scene examination, she confirmed to Mansfield, there was no blood on the floor or walls, no splatter and no bodily fluids, and she said to Mansfield, 'It sounds like a lot of time but there was a large area of house to examine.'

The house was 376 square metres. Matheson's hours were:

Day 1, 1.30 p.m. — 7:45 p.m.
Day 2, 8 a.m. — 8.30 p.m.
Day 3, 8 a.m. — 6.30 p.m.
Day 4, 10 a.m. — 5.30 p.m.
Day 5, 11 a.m. — 4.30 p.m.

Day 6, 9.30 a.m. — 4 p.m.
Day 7, 11 a.m. — 9 p.m.

All for what? In her opening address, Alysha McClintock signalled to the jury that they ought not wait for the ESR evidence with bated breath. 'They tested for blood and things like that within the house, and look, much of that evidence didn't necessarily reveal anything that the Crown relies on,' she said. Strange for the Crown to present its case in the trial of the century with such diffidence. Sometimes I felt that McClintock and Dickey lacked conviction. They sat there for hours and hours as inert presences, as bystanders, two shaggy-haired senior prosecutors with nowt to do, while Mansfield stood up and danced his way through their arguments from those diffident presentations, his shaved head full of ways and means to establish the idea of reasonable doubt. It was his trial. He owned it. I once heard about a distinguished pompous ass in Auckland law who objected to Mansfield being made a silk, or King's Counsel; in a way it was a compliment. He was plainly jealous.

---

The detectives had crept around Polkinghorne's house for eight days. The ESR team had crept around Polkinghorne's house for up to eight hours a day. At the end of week two of the trial, the jury were invited to creep around Polkinghorne's house. A Scene Visit! I have never experienced this rara avis in all my court reporting days and was very excited about it — it was like a school trip, a chance to see the house of horrors, to look and imagine the ghosts of its two former occupants creeping around their own house.

It took considerable planning in chambers for Justice Graham Lang to allow it to proceed. He ordered a security detail of detectives and uniformed police. He choreographed which rooms the jury could see and in what order. He told them: 'Don't touch anything.' He also choreographed which rooms the media could see: none. We had to wait outside. There were further instructions not to photograph him or the lawyers as they got out of their vehicles. I watched the judge and the lawyers as they got out of their vehicles (a VW Golf, a beat-up Toyota), and can exclusively, possibly even lawlessly, report that they get out of their vehicles like everyone else. Still, it was strange to see Justice Lang out from behind the bench. He had shed his black robes. He wore a suit and walked among mere mortals. He even spoke with them. 'Nice haircut,' I said to him; he claimed he had got it cut before I described him in the *Herald* as looking like 'a long-haired wildman of rock'.

The morning of the Scene Visit was a classic day in winter in Auckland: bright, rainless, the harbour blue and flat. The jury were packed into a Pacific Tourways hired minivan (company brochure: 'our fleet ranges from 13 to 53 seats') and driven up through the shopping centre of Parnell Rise (real estate brochure: 'dotted with gift shops and fine-art galleries, each housing incredible pieces ranging from whimsical sculptures to contemporary paintings') then down towards mangrovial tides and playing fields, rising up once more on Shore Road to the border of the golden triangle of Parnell, Ōrākei and Remuera, each of them a zone of gated mansions and gilded cages. The vans parked in front of the city's ultimate gilded cage, chez Polkinghorne (house sale brochure: 'From the moment you open the front gate you sense that you are about to enter a home of substance . . . Meticulously manicured gardens set a scene of peaceful tranquillity.') It was a journey of only 10 kilometres but it brought into view the secret appeal of the Polkinghorne trial: it operated as a portrait of Auckland.

Big, loud, crowded, happy, anxious, nosy, drugged, violent, adorable, shimmering, extremely rich, extremely poor and extremely horny Auckland was the setting and the star of the trial. It presented as everything everyone has ever thought of it as: a South Pacific port made good, a roisterous city of possibilities.

The trial was not a portrait of the Auckland of factories and RESIDENTS PARKING ONLY slums. It was a weird kind of love letter to the city of sales and marketing, money sparkling on the waters of the Waitematā, money lapping towards the sensual hips of Rangitoto, money coming in on the tide and offering itself to the landed gentry of Herne Bay, Mission Bay and Ōrākei Basin. Auckland's power and wealth burn brighter than all of New Zealand's one-horse towns, e.g. Wellington. And so that billet-doux held Polkinghorne gunning his Mercedes-Benz over the harbour bridge every Friday to meet a sex worker on the city's North Shore, and it held witnesses talking about his investment portfolio, his workout regime at CityFitness in Newmarket, his stashes of methamphetamine as photographed in drawers next to Pauline's Clarins body lotion, Elizabeth Arden ceramide capsules, LifeStyles Silky Smooth water-based lubricant (brochure: 'Compatible with latex and polyisoprene condoms') and big black vibrator.

The house was on the corner of a pretty cul-de-sac lined with oak trees and providing intimate views down onto Ōrākei Basin. It was an architecturally designed series of white boxes next door to an architecturally designed series of black boxes. Both were large many-bedroomed spreads, but neither one was as large as the many neighbouring enormous mock-Tudor piles with quaint little attic windows. The streets of the eastern suburbs are paved with gold and lined with oak and conifer, hibiscus and plane; it was a zone of swimming pools and private schools, of Porsches and BMWs; after the Scene Visit, I walked down to the lovely shores of Ōrākei Basin, and along to the shops and cafés of Ōrākei Village, where an orange Porsche 911 Carrera was leaving just as a white Tesla with the licence plate TOLD YOU was arriving. O garish Auckland! Back in the 1980s, the late Stephen Stratford wrote an essay for Auckland's *Metro* magazine, with the classic headline: 'Wellington: why they hate us, and why we pity them'. It's as true now as it was then, and the same sentiment belongs to the rest of New Zealand — everyone hates Auckland, its flash and cash, its good life. Secretly, though, they yearn for it.

A large oak leaf stuck to the wet railings of Polkinghorne's upstairs balcony. The letterbox instructed, 'Address mail only'. There were little conifers and a white camellia and two potted succulents. You could look through the downstairs windows and see an abstract painting in yellows and reds on a wall near the front doorway; it was here that emergency services discovered Pauline's body.

The house was north-facing. You could look through the upstairs window into the bedrooms — it would offer wonderful views of dear old Rangitoto stretching itself out in the harbour — and form morbid pictures of what happened up there on the morning of Easter Monday, 5 April 2021. But really there wasn't much you could look at from the pavement; inside, the jury went through the house, and then it was the turn of the prosecutors and Polkinghorne's lawyers, who included Mansfield's handsome right-hand man Harrison Smith, who sat to Mansfield's left.

The house would look lovelier in summer, with the big pōhutukawa outside it in scarlet bloom, and Ōrākei Basin baked blue in bright sunlight. Auckland, at its best, is not merely a place where some people have a lot of money; it's truly the most beautiful city in New Zealand, a watery, subtropical knock-out, offering good times for everyone on the shores and the islands and the volcanoes and the basins. When I left the Scene Visit, everyone else returned to court, but I decided to take a stroll down to Ōrākei Basin, which was at high tide. There was a ramp for jet skis. Kingfishers flew over the water. I rested on a pontoon on the water and scoffed Woolworths Choccy Fingers — I had offered the packet to the judge, prosecution, defence and the security detail of detectives and uniformed police at the Scene Visit, but they felt they were too good for it — and looked back up to the ridge above the basin, to the house where Pauline Hanna died. The poor woman was 63. She had a lot to live for, but by her own account it had not altogether been a happy life.

CHAPTER 4

# Pauline

We have to talk about Pauline. And we did, incessantly during the eight weeks in courtroom 11, sometimes with excruciating intimacy, sometimes with such forensic violation of her body that her friends fled the court in tears, but sometimes, too, with kindness and fondness, in tribute to a woman who was successful, thoughtful, hard-working, proud, stylish, sexy, vulnerable, smashed, broken, sleepless, loving, loved and lost.

Her death was at the centre of the trial. But even though a likeness of her flickered into view, she felt hard to know; the real Pauline seemed opaque, concealed. She always had her defences up. She was in pain. Her marriage, with its harrowing Ts&Cs, made her feel, among other things, humiliated and ashamed of herself. She was world-class at keeping up appearances. She put on a great front, took considerable pride in it. Everyone commented on how immaculately she dressed; her hair was immaculate, her make-up immaculate. Her self-presentation papered over a multitude of sins, as in her husband's sins, his multitudinous store-bought fuckfest. She smiled and waved, a regal presence concealing the foul rag and bone shop of her trampled, broken heart. There were glimpses of the woman within. The court heard from her doctor, who recited the list of pharmaceutical potencies that she regularly prescribed to Pauline. The court heard from her family and friends, who talked of two Paulines, the relaxed Pauline away from Polkinghorne, the uptight Pauline with Polkinghorne. Mainly, the court heard about Pauline from Pauline herself, in emails and texts that were read out to the court, and we also heard her voice in an extraordinary dinner party. Her family had gathered at Longlands, the Hawke's Bay farm where her brother Bruce lived, and a tape recording was made of her confessions for all eternity: 'Here's the real deal,' she drawled, wise and cynical and battered.

Bits and pieces of memoir were assembled. She grew up on an orchard in Hawke's Bay. She was the middle child between Bruce and their younger sister Tracey. 'I grew up for ever in the shadow of my brother,' she emailed herself in a kind of diary or autobiography; one that was presented by Ron Mansfield during the defence case. She wrote the message in the bad summer of 2018, depressed at the seeming failure of her marriage to Polkinghorne, and its lugubrious, self-loathing tone reads like someone determined to be miserable about everything. It reads like fiction. Just as pride disguises the shambles of our circumstances, pain alters the bland truth of things in favour of drama, trauma, lasting unhappiness, and sets out to chant over and over and over: *No one ever loved me*. The email continued, 'My father loved me first and foremost but for my Mother, Bruce was first and foremost. Tracey, 13 years younger than me, was never in the fray — but Mother erred towards her. Dad died too young to help me [. . .] Throughout my life because I was painfully shy I was continually hurt, cried myself to sleep often, rejected by my girlfriends because I was too timid except when I met Pheas [Victoria Riordan, her closest friend, who went by her amazing middle name, Pheasant] on our Secretarial course.'

Pheasant appeared as a witness for the prosecution. In many ways she was the star witness: she performed the most filmed and photographed action of the entire trial, when she told the court that Pauline confided in her that Polkinghorne had once put his hands around her neck in a rage, and threatened, 'I can do this any time I want.' Pheasant clasped her hands tight around her own neck to mime what Pauline showed her. It was a gotcha moment, a smoking gun — actually I am only saying this because it's what all the other journalists instantly recognised. I was too dozy and insensitive and literal to think much of it. Pauline's death was not caused by strangling her neck in that manner. I shrugged off the demonstration, which Pheasant performed over and over, holding her neck tighter and tighter. I should have regarded it as frightening. The truth is that I regarded it as a bit meaningless. I felt chastised when Alysha McClintock gave her closing address and identified it as 'the single most significant piece of evidence' throughout the entire trial. 'What we know,' said McClintock, 'is that Dr Polkinghorne was willing to attack Pauline by the throat.' Right. Of course. But I just sat there like a dummy at the time of the demonstration and merely took note of Pheasant's beautifully chosen outfit: a two-piece cream suit with antique cameo brooches.

She made a striking, confident, supremely likeable witness, and so, too, did Pauline's close friend Alison Ring, who modelled a groovy trench coat when she gave evidence on the same day. Alison shared a story Pauline told her about how once when she was having sex with Polkinghorne, the phone rang; he picked it up but remained otherwise carnally occupied. Stay classy, Remuera. She also shared a comment Polkinghorne made to her after Pauline's death. 'She wouldn't just fuck one man,' he told her. 'She'd fuck the whole team.' There were numerous times during the trial when Polkinghorne came across as vile. More vileness was to follow, in Ring's evidence. She said he produced what he claimed was a suicide note. My colleagues on the press benches had no other choice than to resort to the lower orders of journalese and describe it as a 'bombshell'. The police had never found one and no one had ever heard of such a thing until Alison's report that he had shown her that piece of paper. Alison dismissed it as a fiction. She didn't have anything to do with him after that.

In cross-examination, Mansfield stood to face Pheasant and Alison, these two women who had the slightly imperious manner and definitely good taste (the antique cameos, the trench coat) of the comfortably-off professional classes, and stared them in the eye, and challenged them, and doubted them, and scolded them, and he . . . ended up with jack. Mansfield can chase veteran cops around a courtroom in a cross-examination but Alison and Pheasant chased Mansfield around courtroom 11, and sent him off the premises. They had the wonderfully secure air of not ever taking any kind of shit.

I became fast friends with Pheasant after that. Following the verdict, she left the court in tears; I was standing against a wall outside the High Court, somewhat stunned, and she walked over and we held each other. She said, 'Write that he got away with murder. You write that. Make sure you write that.' We were photographed; my best side — the back of my head — was in the paper the next day, when we were shown embracing. Someone wrote on social media, 'Shows whose side Steve Braunias was on.' I have no real idea whether Polkinghorne killed his wife but I will always side with Pheasant. I liked her more with each day at the trial, and the more I liked her the closer Pauline came into view. It was possible to imagine these two lifelong friends sharing the same quick, uproarious sense of humour, the same direct approach to life and people, the same feminine elegance.

Pauline's autobiographical email continued, 'Overseas for two years, ended up being 7. Pheas always there. Got home. Dad died. Devastation. Mum shunted us off to do our thing after 2 days! I was at Uni — living with Pheas and John [Riordan, her husband] in year 3. About to fail given my grief but passed with A+ and topped the business school.

'Went to Otago — still really insecure and not able to believe in myself. Ended up with first in class and sent to Montreal and won the International MBA competition of 30 schools. Beat Harvard, Oxford, Cambridge and others.'

Polkinghorne had talked about this achievement with real pride during his three-hour police interview. Detective Walton, bland as ever, responded with a monotonal, 'Wow.'

Pauline's narrative moved to her romantic life. It didn't sound very romantic.

> Came back and got hitched up with Graeme. Lonely time in place — after 10 months in Christchurch followed him to Auckland. I was never "besotted" — and the family did not like him but I persevered.
>
> There were two occasions that made the non-reality of it "real". Christmas. His family came up from Dunedin and stayed with us in our (new) house — I was so miserable — they did not enter the spirit of Christmas, they were so functional, I tried to be loving, they were cold. The second occasion was when I wanted to do some planting around our house — and Graeme said "he just wanted a quiet life" and we had enough and didn't want to change anything. I knew it wasn't me but I did not know how to break it up.

And then the tone changes. Her life was about to become more exciting. She meets a man at a charity event. 'Then Blind Foundation Dinner,' she writes, and types the most important word in her life, her fingers caressing each key, 'Philip.'

---

He was the love of her life, and to her friends and family he was the cause of her death either directly or indirectly, destroying her confidence, driving her to despair — they hated him and always will, always had. 'I know you've never liked Philip,' Pauline said to her family on the Longlands tape. No one voiced a correction.

I could imagine a version of Pauline when I talked with Pheasant, and also when I talked with her brother, Bruce. Bruce's wife, Shelley, always knew it was Pauline when Bruce was on the phone — he would laugh and laugh and laugh; they used humour to overcome obstacles and get on with life.

But I couldn't even imagine her as Polkinghorne's wife whenever I spoke with him. I got no sense of her, no identity. It was all him, he was his own island, a little solitary unit of control and neuroses. He talked about her quite a bit, castigated himself for not listening to her and for failing to register just how depressed she was; it felt empty, or at least useless. In any case I couldn't even picture them together. Probably it was another failure of imagination. Pauline was a passionate, excited presence in her email memoir. She wrote about their first fateful meeting at the Blind Foundation charity dinner in Parnell, where a giant pōhutukawa tree dominates the front garden, festooned with thick aerial roots which hang down like long beards, giving it the romantic appearance of something in a bayou, a mossy American everglade. She writes, 'Monday: Philip ratting on my door and saying "are you talking to me, after the kiss on Friday night. We must have lunch Thursday."

'Me: "I can't. I am partnered."

'Thursday: Said to the taxi driver when we arrived at French Café, "Please take me around the block. I am about to make a decision that is going to affect the rest of my life."

'French Café, Philip took my hand, heart flipping. I was sold and the rest is what we have.'

The illicit romance, the stolen kiss, the graciousness of Auckland's finest restaurant — okay. I can see all that. And I can accept the shape of a long, content marriage. It's easy to imagine their shared years of hilarity and travel, intimacy and gracious living. He, parent of three kids from his first marriage, co-founding Auckland Eye and settling into a successful professional career as an expert in the field of vitrectomy; she, childless but managing his kids, forging her own successful career in public health, holding it together but maybe only just, a captive in her Remuera home and Coromandel summer house, her two gilded cages. There were holidays in Europe to take walking tours and canal tours. Message from Pauline to Polkinghorne: 'There's a new show on Netflix called *Emily in Paris* and she is having lunch at the spot we went to with each other.' They looked cute together; in the terrible portrait of Polkinghorne in the sex maniac costume of red pants with zips in the legs, Pauline is elegant in a fuchsia trouser suit and black sequined sleeveless top.

Her email continues, reaching for locked caps:

> Philip FIRST PERSON IN MY LIFE who loved me first — (even more than my father) — For that I have always been amazed and grateful and loved and warmed and done my utmost to return. We have created a Family. I have also prioritised Polkinghornes over Hannas but that means nothing to Philip.
>
> Philip is my life. We have BOTH been through ups and downs. Amy transitioning to Taine was, and still is, devastating for Philip and he will never adjust — I worked so hard to get Amy/Taine assistance, to broker the relationship to keep everyone safe.
>
> No-one in my life has EVER loved me for me. Philip did that — and Philip is my sole mate. And that is the whole under

> foundation of my life. We have been through some tough times. I thought we were a unit.
>
> I have worked so very hard (as has Philip). But because Philip is my life, that is what I wanted to do — and I have supported his career — he has gone from strength to strength. I thought despite the ups and downs we still love each other and are aligned.

She writes about a bad argument in August 2018:

> What he said to me that night was not only devastating — and there was lots of it — but the key thing that hurt, hurt, hurt, was "Our last 25 years is a waste of time."
>
> It waf incredible I almost (still) cannot take it in.
>
> We have created gorgeous children, two daughters-in-law, a grandson, two beautiful houses, I have finnes/ class — I look good, I represent as the wife of Professor Polkinghorne, I fit in, do the thing.

The occasional errors — 'waf', 'sole', 'finnes' — only emphasise the speed and intensity of her writing; she can't stop, things are spiralling too fast for the pedantries of spellcheck. The slips strengthened Mansfield's argument that Pauline was a danger to herself. The intensity of the email got worse and worse.

> Philip took me out for dinner which was magic (I have been wanting to be with him all weekend). Went to dinner with my boyfriend. All good. I talked too much in the car coming home.

> The rest is ugly and I don't know what to do. Then spend 30 seconds feeding cats before bringing wine upstairs.
>
> Then all hell breaks loose — I have not behaved as he wanted — and I cry — I am gutted, been holding it in for so long. And he is angry and doesn't want to know me or my issues or me for that matter.
>
> HURT HURT HURT — in fact wrecked. All these years (27) did I get it wrong that he was the only person who truly loved me as his number 1. I was number 1 in someone's life — as he was in mine — have we got that wrong?? God what a prospect — I cannot live if that is the result that I got it wrong.
>
> I don't know what to do. I do know that this is not sustainable for Philip or me. I cannot express my love, admiration, return his love and that fact that I treasure the fact that he loves me first, more than all that I have done — I am lost.

But she wasn't lost. She had people who loved her, looked out for her, wanted to look after her. There was good old Pheas and her husband John Riordan; when Pauline showed them how Polkinghorne tightened his hands around her throat, they implored her to pack her bags that instant, leave him, come back with them. There was good old Bruce and his family; in the wretched Longlands recording, they are forever telling her they're there for her, even or especially after she laid it all out in the open:

> Here's the real oil. I used to join the prostitutes and be part of the fucken thing and so I would have been with so many men and dah-dah-dah.

God knows what kind of sex horror was skipped over in that 'dah-dah-dah'. She continued,

> I did that because I wanted to make sure he didn't go off the rails. But now I can't do it any more. Three years ago I decided I can't do this shit. I had to drink two bottles of wine before I go with another man. And it's just revolting. I hate it. I would go to the parties with five or six or seven . . . So now he goes off and screws women when he's away and I take a very foul view of that and he hurts me and I know he loves me. I know he's such a sex fiend and he videos it and I've got the videos . . . He's really hurt me to the extent I've thought why am I living with him.

No one changed the subject at that dinner, no one tried to minimise it out of embarrassment. They let her talk. They *wanted* her to talk. Pauline continued about her husband, the 'sex fiend': 'He's got a sexual appetite that's extraordinary.' And there were statements about his violent temper: 'He's out of control. He doesn't understand how to control himself. He's somebody who gets very, very, very wound up.'

To all of which Bruce says to her, 'You're one of us.'

His wife Shelley says, 'Your brother has got your back.'

'I know that,' Pauline says.

'You should know that,' Bruce says.

'I know I can come home here,' Pauline says. 'I know that.'

Mansfield cross-examined Bruce Hanna after the court was played the tapes of Longlandsgate. He asked Bruce if he knew about an email from Pauline saying that she felt bullied at work and was stressed by her job leading the Covid-19 vaccine response.

'No,' said her brother.

He asked him if he knew she had made a suicide attempt in 1992.

'No,' said her brother.

He asked him if he knew Pauline was on antidepressants, had been referred to a psychiatrist and was diagnosed with alcohol dependency syndrome in 2013.

'No,' said her brother.

There was something four-square and bracingly honest about Bruce. He was asked how he used to get on with his widowed brother-in-law. 'We got on okay,' he said, making okay sound like something stuck to the bottom of his shoes. When he left the courtroom after that, he took no notice of Polkinghorne and walked past him like he didn't exist. It was preferable to knowing he did exist. He really loved his sister. I could see her in *his* eyes. To listen to Pauline at the Longlands dinner is to listen to someone surrounded by a close, loving family, who give her the support she needs, tell her she isn't alone. She sounded strong, comforted. It was weird to hear her voice in open court. She sounded present. You could picture her at the table, gorgeous and frank and at ease. She spoke in a posh kind of drawl, someone forthright, direct, bossy, no one's fool, claiming she was in no way going to put up with living her life as her husband's 'doormat'. But at the same time, she was making very strenuous efforts to lay down and live her life as his doormat. They didn't understand him, she said. 'He's a very complicated person,' she said. 'Please don't hate Philip. He is a good man. He is going through a lot of stress

. . . I'm safe, darling. I'm safe.' And over and over and over: 'I love him. He loves me. I love him. He loves me I love him. He loves me I love him. He loves me.'

She was telling the truth about that; there was someone else other than Pheas and Bruce who loved her, and looked out for, and looked after her — Polkinghorne.

---

South African-born detective Andrew Reeves was tasked with opening Polkinghorne's email and text records, and he duly read or summarised a great many to the court. They weren't all about sex: only approximately 99.9 per cent of them. They were a record of the Remuera burgher gone rogue and rutting. They were a testament to turpitude and tumescence. But they were also selective. In his cross-examination, Mansfield made sure the court heard of other emails and texts that were far more favourable towards Polkinghorne. They revealed a sweet, silly, loving husband; they also revealed a happy, receptive, loving wife.

These were messages after the crisis of the summer of 2019. They were a record of an apparently harmonious marriage throughout 2020 and heading towards Pauline's death in April 2021.

'Hi beautiful lady.'

'Hi darling pie.'

'Are you happy with fish for tea? And salad.'

'Thank you darling.'

'No bread here,' he texts after a visit to the supermarket in the anxious stockpiling days before the first lockdown. 'Half the shelves are empty.'

'Did you see Ashley Bloomfield was pushed under the bus by the health minister?' she reports.

'I am sitting next to Andrew Little,' he writes, flying to Australia after lockdown. She writes to him before his return, 'Have a good flight, good night my darling. I'm going to have a shower.'

He replies, 'I now have a boner.'

Pauline: 'Save it up!'

And on his way home from Auckland airport: 'Security thought I was carrying a pistol in my trousers. I said no but I'm going to see the most gorgeous lady on the planet.'

No hookers. No methamphetamine. No rage. No arguments. No simmering resentment about to boil over into an act of violence. Just the nice exchanges documenting the happy days of their married lives, ordering meals from Shahi in Remuera, watching Netflix (Pauline loved *After Life*, the Ricky Gervais series), taking delight in photographing a wood pigeon in the treetops.

'Happy Valentine's Day!'

'Got you coffee!'

'How's the morning going big boy?'

'Thank God I've got you to come home to.'

'Off to the Churchill Club in Glendowie.'

'Great to hear *FQ* is coming back! Such a great magazine.'

Under Mansfield's instructions, Reeves the South African cop read aloud messages between Mr and Mrs Polkinghorne that were about rack of lamb for dinner, about eye fillet for dinner, about buying nappies for the grandkids, about buying a carpet cleaner, about work: 'Waiting on a fucking patient,' Polkinghorne wrote. On 1 April 2021, Polkinghorne texts her that he has fish for dinner.

On 2 April, Easter Friday, Hanna reports an emergency: Farro Fresh is closed. On 3 April, he texts her, 'Picked up drycleaning and hung out washing. Have you had lunch? Ting me when you are on your way and I can make you poached eggs.' On 4 April, the last day of her life, there is only one text between them. She takes some junk to the rubbish tip, and writes, 'On my way back.' As ever, she adds a row of three love-heart emojis. Happy wife, happy life; but then she drives home, makes dinner (strips of pork), watches Netflix (*New Amsterdam*), and by dawn of Easter Monday, Polkinghorne (wildly unexciting text, 16 February 2020: 'Putting bins out') is a widower.

It was a portrait of surfaces and facades, of masquerades and false impressions. To the Crown, she was only just holding back the pain of a marriage gone to hell; to the defence, she was collapsing under the intolerable pressure of work, of drink, of prescription medicines, of 63 years of low self-esteem. Either version insisted on seeing her as an actress. She was like one of Truman Capote's swans. Capote said of his favourite swan, Babe Paley, that he had never seen anyone more perfect: her posture, the way she held her head, the way she moved. Pauline, too, was an immaculate conception. If she did take her own life, maybe the decision to see herself off the premises of the Earth wearing only a dressing gown, nothing underneath, no effort made to preserve her beauty and her myth, was because she was sick of the pretence, the act. 'Everything the swans do is skin-deep,' Capote patronised. As one of the swans of Remuera life, Pauline closed the curtains and screamed.

The prosecution asked another police officer to read another of Pauline's messages: Madeleine Palmer, a constable training to be a detective. She was the only person to appear in court who was smaller than Polkinghorne. She looked to be in her twenties, and she wore her hair in a ponytail. Just about everyone in her generation speaks with a vocal fry but it gave her reading a strange power; it was as though her voice was breaking, catching on the jagged edges of suffering, as she read from an email Pauline wrote to Polkinghorne when it looked like the two were about to separate. The performance in courtroom 11 sounded like a torch ballad.

Pauline scurried around the page, pleading, begging, in thrall to her lord and master.

> I have never been dirty but take on board your criticism about my handling of food . . . I take my dishes down to the dishwasher in the morning . . . I do shop for groceries, I do shop for things for the house, I do get flowers etc to make it nice . . . I don't wear bodysuits, I don't pick up the glasses by their upper rim etc etc as you keep criticising me . . . I don't ever wear my bodysuits other than to work, I strive to make you proud of my work effort/ethic, I attempt to pre-empt your difficult days by encouraging you when you are in theatre, doing the dinner when I know you are tired, preparing the types of things I think you like.

What's with the bodysuits? What's with the insecurity, the craven attitude, the doormatting? The constable also read from Polkinghorne's letter to Pauline. Even if she had tried to, Palmer couldn't have made the letter sound like a cry from the heart. Its opening sentence was so poorly composed and read so impersonally it was like something written by ChatGPT: 'Dearest

Pauline, I have felt increasing devoid in the last few months from our relationship.'

What? And this awful Grinchy command: 'For many years you have asked what I want for Christmas and my stock answer has been to not ask me to borrow money from me.' Also: 'In 25 years I don't think you have ever paid for the rates, water bill, insurance etc.' Everyone who has ever been in a bad relationship has complained about their partner's unequal contribution to the water bill and knows that they're not actually complaining about that at all: the water bill is a weapon within easy reach to crack the shell of the relationship, to disguise the real inequality of love. Pauline loved too much. Polkinghorne loved too little or not at all. Pauline wrote, 'I still have a bucketload of love and I think you do too.' His reply was cold, like an employer putting someone on notice: 'I don't know what happened to the bucketload of love, but there you have it.'

Their repetitions of a 'bucketload of love' sound like something they always used to say to each other, was part of their lovers' language, their secret code. Polkinghorne withdrew it. This is the Pauline I can see: a mess, weeping, empty-handed. All that was left was shopping.

---

An expenses spreadsheet was produced at court. There is something grubby about it — it goes through Pauline's pockets, follows her around — but economic law states that we are what we spend. Her 2020 expenses are a map of an Auckland woman's middle-class life in the eastern suburbs, a big spender but not foolishly so, buying things for the home, fixing her hair, fixing her skin, forever steaming her clothes at Regal Drycleaners. Emporiums become part of a city's soul. There she is at Smith & Caughey's, the beloved Auckland department store now a shadow of itself. There she is at Margaret's at Heretaunga Street West in Hastings, where it stood for 43 years until closing in late 2020. 'I love people,' owner Margaret McLean said in a farewell interview with *Hawke's Bay Today*. 'I love dealing with mature ladies because they are sincere in what they want.'

Here is an itemised rundown of what Pauline sincerely wanted in the first three months of 2020.

January 9, 2020: Farmers, $110
January 9: Trelise Cooper, $540
January 11: Gregory women's clothing in Newmarket, $150
January 12: Regal Drycleaning, $406.40
January 14: Palm Clinic, $880
January 24: Farmers, $233.98
January 25: Malo restaurant in Havelock North, $533
January 26: Farmers in Hastings, $171.49

February 2: Farmers, $467.18
February 2: Farmers, $151.90
February 7: Regal Drycleaning, $520.75
February 7: Regal Drycleaning, $93.50
February 13: Bendon in Manukau, $212.88
February 15: Headquarters salon in Remuera, $283
February 16: Farmers, $166.99
February 19: Gregory, $419

February 20: Gregory, $269
February 20: About Face facials in Herne Bay, $159
February 22: Farmers in Hastings, $156.16
February 22: Margaret's women's clothing in Hastings, $229.75

March 1: Karen Walker, $130
March 5: Regal Drycleaning, $133.90
March 5: Headquarters, $367
March 10: About Face, $159
March 19: Farmers, $146.93
March 19: Regal Drycleaning, $455.70
March 24: Rodney Wayne, $362
March 24: Farmers, $530.96

---

Headquarters in Remuera was owned and managed by Anne Millar for 27 years. Pauline came into the Walton Street salon every four weeks for 25 of those years. Anne thought she always looked immaculate. Pauline's hair, her nails, her clothes, her make-up — all of it perfect. Anne thought that for a woman of her age, 63, Pauline had an amazing figure. 'I've got plenty of men after me,' Pauline said at that Longlands dinner. 'I've actually got quite a lot of men who fancy me quite frankly. I'm fucken hot.'

She asked for a tint. Anne put on a L'Oréal product and told Pauline she would be back in 35 minutes while it processed. Pauline immediately took a Zoom call with her staff at Counties Manukau District Health Board. She had a senior role, responsible for the vaccine roll-out to combat Covid in Auckland, and she couldn't afford to waste a minute. Sometimes she emailed throughout the night. It was a stressful job — truly dealing with matters of life and death — and sometimes it got too much. She messaged herself twelve months before she died:

> I have worked 15/16 hours over Easter. I am never good enough despite my efforts — today is the 25th day of work in a row — but I am not adding any value. I want desperately to tell someone and cry and ask for help . . . I must stand on my own two feet but I don't know if I have two feet or what they look like . . . So I have had three glasses of wine and a beautiful dinner thanks to PJP [Polkinghorne] — but I don't know what to do with myself. So I will go to bed and not sleep. Very unusual for me — and it builds up — who knows what might follows. Have to tell someone even if no one but God ever sees this.

She knew she drank too much. At least one bottle of wine most evenings for the last ten years, she told her doctor. The doctor appeared as a witness at the trial and rather blithely confirmed the rate and regularity of prescribing Pauline antidepressants and appetite- and alcohol-craving suppressants: Prozac, Duromine, naltrexone, disulfiram and fluoxetine. The doctor was cross-examined by Hannah Stuart, who made a very refreshing substitute for Mansfield. Stuart read out Pauline's medical records.

'June 17, 2019. More Prozac.'

The doctor, who clung to name suppression: 'Yes.'

'July 1. More Duromine.'

'Yes.'

'September 20. More Prozac.'

'Yes.'

'September 25. More Duromine.'

'Yes . . . '

Pauline had always made appointments at Headquarters on Thursday nights. Covid changed everything, and she now made bookings for Saturdays. After the Zoom meeting, Anne came back and blow-dried Pauline's hair. It was Waitangi Day. Pauline asked Anne what her plans were that night, and Anne said she was hosting a dinner party. Pauline paid on her way out, and then came back a few minutes later with a beautiful bouquet of flowers to give Anne for her table at the dinner party.

There were two more hair appointments after that, and both times Pauline worked throughout on her laptop. She worried about putting on weight, and she took prescription medicine for that. She worried about sleeping, and took prescription medicine for that, too. 'I don't know how you hold it all together,' she was told at the Longlands dinner. Pauline replied, 'No, sometimes I don't either.'

There were other anxieties. Her internet searches included 'anorgasnia' (a misspelling of 'anorgasmia', the difficulty of reaching orgasm) and 'what does it feel like to smoke methamphetamine'. She had a restless intelligence; her other various searches included *Struggle Without End* by Māori historian Ranginui Walker, and authors such as Julian Barnes, Zola, Flaubert, Proust, Oscar Wilde (and, strangely, 'Oscar Wilde wife'). She loved extremes — letting the bathroom steam up into a fog before she showered, opening all the windows in the house to let in the cold air. Her breakfast was always the same — one piece of toasted MacKenzie bread with Olivani and Rose's lime marmalade.

Polkinghorne said she was the only person he knew who could drink a cup of tea while lying down in bed. Well, she had to do something to occupy herself; according to Polkinghorne's long-term lover, Madison Ashton, he would pound away at his wife for 45 minutes every morning. Another version of their lovemaking routine came from Alison Ring: 'Pauline would lie back and pretend she was sleeping. Then he would bring her marmalade on toast.'

She made idle, happy chatter whenever she saw Anne at Headquarters. Her attitude was positive. Pauline was a striking, generous woman, with good friends — she regularly caught up for coffee with a cohort of professional women who called themselves the Housewives of Middlemore. She was open with them about her husband's 'extraordinary sex drive'. During her marriage crisis in 2019, she had the idea that Polkinghorne was in talks with Simon Blackwell, said to be the best divorce lawyer in Auckland. But the couple stayed together and their messages to each other during the day throughout 2020 and early 2021 were frequent and affectionate.

Anne Millar said in the witness box that she last saw Pauline on 20 March 2021. The appointment was for 2.30 p.m. Pauline arrived ten minutes late. 'She was busy and distracted with her work throughout,' Anne said. But she told Anne she was looking forward to a 4WD holiday in the South Island with friends. Pauline rushed off at 3 p.m. to have a Zoom meeting in her car.Anne only had time to give her hair a quick blast on the way out.

'See you again soon,' Anne said to one of her best customers.

'See you then,' said Pauline, and walked to her Mercedes. She got in, made calls, replied to emails, and drove off closer towards her doom.

January 9, 2021: Regal Drycleaners, $763.87
January 9: Regal Drycleaners, $141
January 12: Headquarters, $230
January 21: Shampoo 'n' Things, $165
January 21: Sass & Bide women's clothing in Newmarket, $396
January 23: David Jones, $186
January 23: Regal Drycleaners, $264.30
January 23: Regal Drycleaners, $64
January 25: Smith & Caughey's, $127
January 27: Ricochet women's clothing in Newmarket, $173.40

February 9: Headquarters, $275
February 13: Shampoo 'n' Things, $110
February 13: David Jones, $110
February 13: Regal Drycleaners, $331.20
February 27: Headquarters, $235

March 9: Rodney Wayne, $155
March 9: Smith & Caughey's, $1544
March 11: Cos in Commercial Bay, $353
March 13: Smith & Caughey's, $175
March 18: Smith & Caughey's, $617
March 20: Headquarters, $280

April 1: Palm Clinic, $1496
April 3: Sandro, $402

CHAPTER 5

# Polkinghorne Shops at the Sex Supermarket

As the trial progressed, the awesome power of the state picked up pace, its resources and vittles packed into a wagon that rode across the prairies of courtroom 11, seeking to crush the bones of Polkinghorne's defence to dust. There was something thrilling about the industrial judiciary complex at work. A blank cheque accommodated such labours as those 53 hours that ESR scientist Fiona Matheson billed for combing the Polkinghorne home from 8 a.m.– 8.30 p.m., etc. To behold the return of Brian Dickey each morning was to witness a heavyweight boxer return to the Crown ring; while together, Dickey and McClintock led an invading force that set out to shock and awe. The watching public in the High Court were duly shocked and awed. Courtroom 11 was seldom less than full. People kept on coming every day, filing through the heavily manned X-ray stations at the front doors, queuing for pies and coffees at the real nerve centre of the High Court of Auckland: QC's café. The court café is resistant to the time and tide of history, to the bloodlines of royal succession, and retains its name. Every silked lawyer in New Zealand has gone from QC to KC since the death of Queen Elizabeth and the ascension of King Charles — but not the High Court café. It's tucked away in a dark little alcove on the ground floor and there are signs advising against talking openly about cases. It has the hush of a library. Everyone heads there at some point; the call of a sausage roll is the great leveller of criminal justice; and it was at QC's that the Polkinghorne trial was discussed intently, sotto voce, by the regulars whose attendance gave the whole enterprise an extra, welcome depth. Justice must be seen to be done. They were the seers.

Faces became familiar. There was the nice lady from Howick, there was the nice lady from Raglan, and there was the nice lady with dyed red hair who wore snappy little two-piece suits with gold trim, who had moved as a widow from Whangārei to an apartment in Ponsonby, knew no one in Auckland, but formed a whole new gang of pals courtesy of the Polkinghorne trial. There was also a strange woman who kept to herself. She wore black skirts, black tights, Doc Martens and a backpack; she looked as though she were on her way to work. A conversation with her on the very last day of the trial revealed that she regarded the court as her office.

There was even a school visit. A teacher performed miracles in corralling a herd of Year 11 criminology students from Edgewater College. Year 11! That's very young for a murder trial, but what better lesson in open justice than the Polkinghorne spectacle? The kids had excellent manners and were very respectful. But generally speaking there is no such thing as a silent teenager and during morning recess the Year 11s chatted and hooted and laughed, filling the usually subdued and deeply boring High Court with loud good spirits.

So, too, did the adults. Unlike the kids that same day, though, they had the bad grace to continue yapping and gossiping and happily chuntering on and on as they filed into the courtroom. Something about the presence of so many schoolkids lightened the mood. No one heard the registrar's command to stand for His Honour the King's judge. Justice Graham Lang sat down and patiently waited for them to shut the hell up. The wild animals eventually ceased their howlings.

Shortly afterwards the Edgewater corral shuffled back out of the courtroom. Their teacher led them away: the subject had turned from something more taboo and corrupting than death: sex. It wasn't as if the timing of their school trip was unfortunate. Pretty much every day of the four-week Crown case was immersed in sex. Group sex, daily sex, lots of sex; but the main genre of sex was sex-worker sex. Polkinghorne was an employer who kept sex employees in work. This was confirmed in sex documents.

One morning in the second week I asked the *Herald*'s court reporter Craig Kapitan if I could have a look at the Crown's photo booklet. In his unofficial role as head boy of the reporting school, he held all the available documents in a tidy pile; it lay between himself and the head girl, *Stuff*'s court reporter Cat Owen. They ran the show. They earned that responsibility. They came to court every day of the year; the rest of us were Polkinghorne dilettantes, visiting ghouls with our ghoulish faces pressed up against the glass, ghoulishly. Craig passed the booklet. 'Make sure you give it back,' Cat hissed. And then Craig passed another set of papers. 'We can't report on them yet. But I think you'll find them interesting.' Craig has a restrained and humble manner. His smile stays well within the bounds of his ears and yet it expresses great happiness. The papers he shared were the sex documents.

They were prepared by forensic accountant Margaret Skilton. She had gained access to Polkinghorne's banking records. Skilton duly appeared in the witness box wearing a black and white striped dress above knee-length boots, and read from the sex documents, which enumerated Polkinghorne's spending on sex workers. The main beneficiary was Madison Ashton. Polkinghorne gave her $106,000 in 32 bank transfers; the last payment was for $5580 on 5 January 2021, three months before Pauline's death. He gave $35,905 from 2016 to 2019 to a sex worker named Lee. He gave $61,800 between 2016 and 2021 to a sex worker named Alaria. There were also amounts of $72,100 and $13,550 given to two other people known only by their surnames. Dickey asked Skilton, 'We should say these are all females, aren't they?' Skilton looked up from her Excel songsheets, turned her heart-shaped face towards Dickey, and said, 'Yes.' Oh, and Polkinghorne's cash withdrawals in a single year included $49,000 in 2019 and $84,100 in 2020, in New Zealand, and $142,270 was withdrawn in 2020 from his Australian account . . . I love adding sums and took away Craig's sex documents to run the numbers of Polkinghorne's spend on

Madison, Lee, Alaria and the other payees ('all females') — arriving at $296,646.23.

At the very least it was like a hobby that had got out of hand, at worst, it was a pastime that resembled a long sickness of the soul. But why present it to the court, and place it as evidence for the jury to consider? What was the point of all that? How was it, you know, apropos? They were the record of the lust-funds of a lively little left-handed fellow busily applying himself to living his best libidinous life. It made for great copy — Craig was right, of course; I found the sex documents very interesting indeed, and was proud of myself for making the calculation of $296,646.23 while other media lazily rounded it out to $300,000 — but not for the first or last time it struck me that the Crown itself was running the whole trial as a tabloid exercise. It was the Crown that guised up as sooty-faced, malnourished paperboys on street corners, shrieking, 'READ ALL ABOUT IT!'; it was the Crown that assumed the role of press barons, in the tradition of Hearst and Murdoch and Horton, throwing ink at 72-point headlines that were sure to include the word SEX.

---

I came into possession of another document — prised from the cold hands of Craig and Cat — on Day 1 of the trial. It was the Witness List. The Crown always share it; the defence, never, holding on to it like a secret. It contained 60 names, making it more of a Witness Omnibus, a Witness Directory of Auckland life — New Zealand's biggest city is really still a village, and everyone knew someone scheduled to appear as a witness in five degrees of separation or less. As well as police, first responders, and experts in ropes, pathology, IT and ophthalmology, there were people from civilian life. They included a personal trainer, a hairdresser, and a private investigator who said everything in an almost impossibly sexy whisper. The witness list also included Polkinghorne's housekeeper. I recognised the name in an instant: Sheryl Morris, who co-owned Pagan Records in the eighties and nineties and was one of the great beauties of the age. Pagan had stacks of hits by such as Shona Laing (the poignant 'Glad I'm Not a Kennedy'), Ardijah, Greg Johnson, Tex Pistol and others. Sheryl was New Zealand pop music royalty. Even so, one other name stood out more on the Witness List. It was stardust, golden, magical, a unicorn from the fabled lands of Australia — Madison Ashton.

Madison Ashton! *The* Madison Ashton. No one in New Zealand had ever heard of her until a *Herald* newspaper exclusive — by the irrepressible Carolyne Meng-Yee, inevitably — linked her to Polkinghorne: 'A high-class Australian escort says she is helping police investigate the sudden and unexplained death of Remuera woman Pauline Hanna.' It was published before police charged Polkinghorne with murder. The introduction of Ashton to the narrative came as, you know, a bombshell. She was described as the former mistress of the late Australian cardboard billionaire Richard Pratt. A cardboard billionaire! She said that she met Polkinghorne in 2011 when he and Pauline paid for a $3600 'sex romp' at the Sydney Hilton during a holiday in Australia. A sex romp! Everything about Ashton is spelled in tabloid exclamations. She also claimed they continued a threesome arrangement for several years until Polkinghorne started booking her for solo sessions, and that he took the relationship 'from business to personal' in 2017; her story was that she and Polkinghorne were setting up a home together in Sydney, in an apartment, but she was unaware that he and Pauline were still living together. They rendezvoused on 30 April 2021, at a 'luxury $1725-a-night lodge' in Mount Cook Village. Police raided their room, interrupting the couple sharing a 'romantic room service dinner and drinking champagne' (as per Meng-Yee's exclusive story). It was 25 days after Pauline's death.

Not true that the press corps were beside ourselves with excitement at Madison's imminent arrival at the quaint old High Court of Auckland to give evidence against Polkinghorne. We were beside each other to try and *stabilise* our excitement. It gave the trial an air of comedy, of bedroom farce, the mistress of a cardboard billionaire, about to say who knows what about sex romps. She was due to appear in Week 3 of the trial. One day I asked Mansfield's right-hand man, Harry Smith, whether he was dreading her appearance; he affected an indifference, and mentioned she was expected the following Wednesday. I henceforth made it my business to advise Jan (the nice lady from Howick), Robbyn (the nice lady from Raglan) and Lois (the nice lady from Ponsonby in Whangārei) to be sure not to miss coming to court that day. I could not tell them why — a Witness List is a sacred document — but took considerable pleasure in insisting on it. 'But I have a hair appointment that day,' said Jan. 'You must cancel it,' I gravely instructed.

In the meantime, confirmation of the 30 April rendezvous was supplied in court when Detective Senior Sergeant Lisa Anderson was called to the witness box. She didn't really have much to say other than to confirm that she and two detectives from Christchurch knocked on the door of the Matariki Room of the Mt Cook Lakeside Retreat on 25 April. It was shocking enough: Pauline dead, Pauline buried, Madison booked, all in the same month. Polkinghorne answered the door; the police seized the couple's cellphones; Ashton said later that she was wearing a black catsuit.

All of which ramped up the anticipation of her grand appearance at the High Court of Auckland. She had already drifted into the public imagination as a kind of dark Other; she was bold, overt, larger than New Zealand life; she was a reminder of the tense way we receive visitors from foreign shores, as examined in Damien Wilkins' vastly entertaining 2002 essay, published as a small booklet, *When Famous People Come to Town*. He studies visits by the Royals, Rudyard Kipling, Anna Pavlova, Noël Coward, Yehudi Menuhin, The Beatles, and, in Wellington in 1983, The Birthday Party (Nick Cave and his band were 'put in the dingy Cambridge Hotel'). Madison Ashton wouldn't seem out of place in this queue at the arrivals lounge. Wilkins observes, 'The visits of the famous are always connected with our anxieties.' We are such a small nation. We are so distant. 'Last Lamppost in the World,' Wilkins capitalises, although 'not quite the last stop. That privilege belongs to Antarctica.' New Zealand is 'the portal to the ice'. We stand on the edge of the world, trembling against the cold Antarctic polar blasts; but it's the isolation that really gets into our bones. You could sense a nervousness in courtroom 11 at the prospect of Madison's arrival. Stravinsky toured here in 1961; his assistant Robert Craft kept a diary, and Wilkins quotes from a passage of their stay at the St George Hotel in Wellington: 'Coffee is not served at night, but only tea, and the other way around at noon.' How would Madison's visit disrupt the narrow codes of our island life?

We waited and wondered. As for the New Zealand sex workers implicated in the Polkinghorne trial, they kept their heads down. We were told their working names and given receipts of payments for services rendered. Otherwise, they were vague, discreet presences, going about their private business. We did not hear from them, but we did hear about them. The first witness to say anything on that subject was a barber. Paul Adriaanse had a curious career arc. He had gone from being a mental health clinician to cutting hair for people from his home, a unit in Remuera. His incarnation at the Polkinghorne trial was as a character from opera. Rossini's great work *The Barber of Seville* sheds light on the less than exemplary behaviour of the barber's wealthy clients; Adriaanse, the barber of Remuera, told the court that he met Polkinghorne ('Phil') through a woman at their gym. 'Lee was a prostitute,' he explained, 'and Phil paid to have sex with her.'

Yes, that's generally how that transaction works; and as knee-booted forensic accountant Margaret Skilton told the court, payments to Lee totalled $35,905. But how did Adriaanse know, Brian Dickey asked him when he led evidence in chief, that Lee was a sex worker? There are some things that witnesses are forbidden from saying. Justice Lang had made certain rulings in regard to the barber's appearance. Adriaanse could only reply: 'I *know*.'

Dickey had a bad cold on the day Adriaanse appeared in the witness box. The prosecutor held a tissue pressed to his snoot, and asked Adriaanse whether he met Polkinghorne after Pauline's death. He said he had. He came home one day to find Polkinghorne waiting for him.

'I'd heard about the murder charge, and he'd been arrested, and what have you, and I asked him, "What the hell happened?" He was really upset. He just said that he'd been advised to say nothing, and that I should probably say nothing too. And I said, "Well, I don't know if they're going to come and see me or not, but I don't have anything to hide."'

Dickey asked him what he thought Polkinghorne meant about not talking to police. He answered, 'It was about Lee.'

The ophthalmologist and the mental health clinician turned barber, white men in Remuera, two Kiwi boomers of pension age, talking of death and grief and secrecy and transparency and sex workers; Dickey sniffed into his tissue, and asked, 'And then what happened?'

He said Polkinghorne sat down, and he cut his hair.

---

There is not so much a thin line between the deep New Zealand sense of neighbourliness and the equally profound state of New Zealand nosiness as there is a line that crosses over and back again, a Venn diagram that takes in social responsibility, concern for the welfare of others, and a genetically ingrained flair for surveillance and tittle-tattling.

Two representatives of this conflicted New Zealand mind were called to the witness box on the same day, to speak of Polkinghorne's appointments with a sex worker who lived in an upstairs apartment of a renovated twelve-room motel, just across the harbour bridge on Auckland's North Shore.

She was sometimes known as Rachel and sometimes known as Alaria. She was in her forties and lived with her son. She was thought to be an alcoholic. She received $55,850 in bank transfers from Polkinghorne. But other than these thin biographical details, she stayed in the shadows of the trial, unnoticed — unlike Polkinghorne, who was keenly noticed by two of her neighbours.

The first neighbour called to the witness box was Rob Masters. He was a bearded, wide-shouldered man in excellent shape. He was a fitness instructor, he said, and held classes outdoors in the carpark — it never rains on the North Shore. He started noticing Polkinghorne in December 2019. Polkinghorne established a routine of arriving on Friday afternoons. 'Could be an hour, hour and a half, sometimes it could be longer, you might come out later and see the car still there or it'd be gone.' Polkinghorne was always dressed impeccably but one time he arrived wearing hospital scrubs. 'He would often have like a shoulder bag, which from my eye looked like a shopping bag with women's clothing in it, maybe underwear, something along those lines.' In cross-examination, Mansfield asked him if he was blessed with X-ray vision. He said he was not. How, then, could he see inside the shopping bags? They looked like the kinds of shopping bags that contained lingerie, he answered. 'Or he would have alcohol, champagne.' He said Polkinghorne was obviously absent during Auckland's Level 4 Covid-19 lockdown of 2020 but returned the very next day after it was reduced to Level 3: 'It was like, oh yup, that didn't take long.' In any case it was hard not to recognise Polkinghorne's car. There was Masters, strong and able, instructing his class to feel the burn in the carpark, looking up to see a big white Merc with the licence plate RETINA.

The next witness was Myra Riddington. In the weeks that followed, memories of her brought a smile to the face of everyone in courtroom 11, as we reminisced of that tall, slender lady with white hair and a wonderfully louche physical grace. She sloped in wearing long pale trousers and a long pale top; she made you think of Meryl Streep as Karen Blixen in *Out of Africa*, independent and imperious, dressed for equatorial heat in cool linens and cottons. 'I had a farm,' she seemed to be drawling, 'in Northcote.' When she wasn't talking about Polkinghorne, she was talking about her garden. She saw Polkinghorne when she was gardening. She saw other clients of Rachel's when she was gardening. 'Rachel had a number of clients. Some of them were very nice and friendly. I'd often be in the garden and they might chat about the garden.' Mansfield's opening question was delivered in a sarcasm so thick you could imagine it wilting the plants in Riddington's garden: 'You must have a very beautiful garden, do you?' She replied, in her typically loud, booming voice, 'Yes, I do, thank you.'

Who were Masters and Riddington, these two watchers on the Shore? Mansfield busted out another of his withering sarcasms. 'It sounds like the neighbourhood watch is quite strong in your apartment.' Masters said he used to be a policeman: it was just a habit to keep an eye on the citizenry. 'Twenty years in the police will generally make you quite observant.' As for Riddington, she seemed to be coming from a place of vigilance and eccentricity. Her version of Polkinghorne's visits was at odds with Masters'. She claimed Polkinghorne saw Rachel at least four times a week. Sometimes, she said, he stayed the night. But she shared Masters' memory of seeing Polkinghorne in his hospital scrubs, and she likewise saw him bringing bottles of booze: 'The good kind,' she said, with contempt. She said Rachel was an alcoholic. It was impossible for her to say no to Polkinghorne's largesse. Riddington also shared a valuable insight: 'He's a man who likes to stand out.' The bottles of champagne, the scrubs, RETINA — he did nothing to conceal his visits, parked in broad daylight, announcing himself as the little medico with big swinging-dick energy. His white Merc, his mad socks — before his arrest, after his arrest, it made no difference, he was consistently and exclusively Polkinghorne.

Evidence, then, was heard in regard to Polkinghorne seeing a sex worker called Lee, and a sex worker called Rachel; the narrative of the Crown case was steadily working towards Madison Ashton giving evidence in the witness box. You wondered what it would do to Polkinghorne to sit there and see his former lover make her entrance and then spill whatever lurid beans. You wondered what electric charge would fill the courtroom and connect with our anxieties. You wondered what she would wear. The suspense built and built; police detective Andrew Reeves helped to finesse the suspense when he sat in the witness box and gave synopses of the sex videos on Polkinghorne's phone. 'A woman I identified as Madison Ashton is performing a sex act. There are actually two separate videos of that.' He also reported on looking at pictures of her in lingerie. 'She has a very large social media following and tends to take a lot of promotional images of herself in lingerie.' There was a sex video of Madison performing an act on herself at the same time and on the same date as Polkinghorne performing an act on himself. 'The significance of Dr Polkinghorne's act is that I recognised it as his own house.'

And so the reason for the Crown's sleazy tabloid approach was made clear. The motive behind watching the sex video, and reporting on it, was that it made the same point as the Crown reporting on all of Polkinghorne's shopping at the sex supermarkets of New Zealand and Australian prostitution: that his marriage to Pauline was a sham, he was only committed to acting out his dream of himself as Priapus of the ancient Hellenes, slinging it all over town in twenty-first century form, with a constant inflamed erection and an increasing, teeth-grinding methamphetamine need and a you-do-you-Boo mania so extreme that it drove him mad, drove him to kill his wife, and then have the skill and audacity to cover his tracks. Madison Ashton would have something to say about all this. Madison Ashton was not well disposed towards Polkinghorne. Madison Ashton — a voluptuary, with her wild hair and cosmetic alterations, mining the natural resources of her body, wit and charm in exchange for income from cardboard billionaires and eye surgeons — would present as the highly sexualised motive.

The only problem was that Madison Ashton went missing. The day of her scheduled appearance in courtroom 11 came and went. So did the next day, and the day after that . . . I asked Brian Dickey what the blazes was going on. He said she had ceased contact. The police couldn't find her. She might be in London; she definitely wasn't in New Zealand. I asked Detective Senior Sergeant Chris Allan. I may as well have asked the wall. The wall might have had better skill at finding the missing witness; it was really not very surprising that Operation Kian had lost her and could not locate her. At the very least it seemed like a carelessness.

She never did appear as a witness. The tension in courtroom 11 slackened; we were stuck within the narrow island of New Zealandness, without any disruptive or liberating force from the Australian continent; the famous person did not come to town. 'Hi Steve,' she emailed. 'I'm in Morocco.'

CHAPTER 6

# Madison

Madison Ashton — her stage name a cute transposition of Ashley Madison, the hook-up site for extramarital affairs — sent me a number of very candid, very frank, very damning emails throughout the trial. If she'd disclosed the contents in the witness box, I suppose it might possibly have made all the difference to the verdict, but I think it's just as likely that whatever she said would not have amounted to a hill of beans. The real action in the trial, in the matter of the death of Pauline Hanna, 63, was in the forensics, the physical clues of a life extinguished, the damage or lack of damage to skin and artery and tissue. Madison Ashton was elsewhere when Pauline died. She had nothing to contribute.

And yet, and yet; she was quite plainly going to be the Crown's star witness, the voluptuous sum of a tidy equation — Polkinghorne minus Pauline equals a new life with Madison. She was his motive to get rid of his wife. A man will kill for beauty. A man will kill for lust. A man will kill and try to get away with it for the holy grail of love.

I first heard from Madison after she read one of my daily trial despatches online at the *Herald*. I was receiving a lot of correspondence for these diaries; it felt like the whole nation was plugged into the Polkinghorne socket, and parts of the nation were constantly coming up to me on the street and saying, 'Love your work! Anyway, he's guilty.' Everyone thought it. Everyone wanted him to go down. In that respect, Madison was no different; but while the peasantry were only going on the reporting of a shockorific trial and their own disgust for a short upstart slinging it all over hooker town, Madison came from the position of someone who knew Polkinghorne better than anyone alive. One of my reports began:

> Another day in the trial of the century until another educated professional from the better side of the tracks is accused of murder in even more lurid circumstances, another hooker. The nation that can produce someone as wholesome as a Dame Lisa Carrington can also produce a Polky. 'He screws prostitutes when he's in Sydney,' his wife Pauline told her family; texts were read out in court today from Sydney sex worker Madison Ashton.

The author of those texts emailed that evening:

You keep referring to me as a sex worker, which is my occupation but I was in a de facto relationship with Philip and you've never once just said de facto partner Madison Ashton, also we were engaged so I could be referred to as ex fiancé Madison.

The crown prosecution have maintained their one-dimensional stance on me. Same goes for the incompetent New Zealand police.

The prosecution and the New Zealand police refuse to see me as a loving girlfriend. I am literally Pauline 2.0. Except I was more educated on covert malignant narcissistic men.

Really appreciate it if you actually referred to me as his de facto partner. At least that is accurate for the timeframe.

Police and the prosecution have made so many serious mistakes with my evidence and they literally refused to use the bulk of my really damming evidence. I honestly put my life on the line to go get some of that stuff. It's like they don't want me to succeed, lest it remove some of the sparkle from them.

I doubt he will be convicted. And the police want to do everything to distract from the mistakes they made initially and have done everything to smokescreen and protect themselves.

I feel so sad about the whole situation with Pauline and me. We were both victims of narcissistic domestic abuse.

Regards, ex de facto partner Madison Ashton.

Engaged! Hm. There was no record of that subject in all of their messaging that the police intercepted. As for being in a de facto relationship, although they never actually lived together, they certainly talked about it, and they were planning a life so domestic and so bland that Polkinghorne bought her a washing machine. I wrote in the next day's diary of the trial, 'A brief summary of the Crown case is that Polkinghorne killed his wife to live in de facto bliss with sex worker Madison Ashton and her many Chihuahuas.' Madison was happy with that. Another satisfied reader.

We continued our correspondence throughout the trial. At the same time, she was feeding information to Carolyne Meng-Yee (inevitably), as well as Paula Penfold at *Stuff*. She believed in keeping all lines of communication open — except for the line that led to the High Court of Auckland. She went on the run, sort of, to London, Morocco, Greece, Paris. Interpol were alerted. Interpol! Penfold reported after the verdict, '*Stuff* understands a summons had been issued and repeated efforts by New Zealand police and their counterparts in Australia had been made. There was also a request for help to Interpol but Ashton could not be found.'

What a disaster. Madison blamed the cops for it, felt disrespected, mucked around. Damien Wilkins writes in his 2002 meditation, 'Hostility toward the famous — there should be a study of it which works through the different grades of resistance and aggression.' Maybe something of that sort was at work when police busted Polkinghorne and Madison at their Mount Cook love shack. She told Paula Penfold, 'If they'd done a far better job, i.e. getting me on side from the start, this whole process would've been so much better for everybody involved.' Something nagged at her, though, in many of the emails she sent to me: regret. She could have played a crucial role in court but made the decision to stay away.

Towards the end of the trial, I emailed her, 'It's hard to guess what the verdict will be. The forensics definitely favour reasonable doubt, and not guilty. What do you think?'

She replied:

> When I gave my last statement to the police in late 2023, I asked them specifically if the forensics are watertight. They said they were. Which is an absolute fucking lie. All the concerns I had gathered over the last few years played out in this court case. I am absolutely horrified at the NZ system.
>
> Bringing up all the sex workers was really not necessary, no one leaves a marriage to go off to live with a full-time sex worker as a client. But men leave relationships and murder their intimate partners to go off into another full-time relationship.
>
> I think it's unlikely that he will be convicted, but that still doesn't interfere with my absolute wish for him to be unanimously found guilty.
>
> Everything hinges on did that contraption that he described and assembled be convincing enough for a jury to find him not guilty.
>
> It's so frustrating that Philip is a pathological liar. Philip murdered Pauline to be with me and that is a fact.
>
> This case turned out to be literally circumstantial, I am pivotal to this but I'm still portrayed as 1 dimensional sex worker.
>
> Philip gave me several bottles of Zopiclone, and that stuff works just like Xanax yeah you build up a resistance but it's still works brilliantly especially when it's with one glass of wine. You are out cold. I remember many times getting up to

go to the bathroom on ⅓ of a tablet and I would be staggering, sliding against the wall to make it to the toilet. And then lurch back to bed.

This was not a violent murder. It was passive strangulation.

None of which could ever have been admitted as evidence on account of the fact it was not anything resembling evidence. He emails were big on proclamations, but every now and then she stated a fact. One day I wrote about the Crown's evocation of Polkinghorne as a methamphetamine addict. Madison responded, 'Your latest instalment brought back memories of Philip being high on crystal meth and how much fun he was. He would dance around in my Camilla pink gown, exactly like a fabulous elderly gay man.'

There was a tenderness to that email. It reads like they shared some kind of love. I wrote back, 'You guys sound like you had heaps of fun & you really did seem to love the old queen. How come you parted?'

'That can't be a serious question Steve,' she answered.

'Well, the last I ever read of your relationship together was that you seemed real happy to meet him at Mount Cook three weeks after Pauline's death. Things seemed all good up until then. Did he basically at some point straight-up confess?'

Her next reply was detailed.

Straight up confess no, but I put it to him that he killed her twice and he agreed, and I also asked him why he did it and he said he didn't know.

I put that to the police. They didn't think it very good so

> I asked for their help to wear a wire and what to say and they didn't want to assist me.
>
> If they had just told me Philip was married and stopped me from going to Mount Cook, they could've spared me that stupid raid and I would've given everything over willingly had I known the situation but I honestly thought they were harassing my partner. Pauline legitimately killed herself. Phillip was my only source of information.
>
> I went out of my way to get that admission of guilt, specially because I thought there's a chance he might try and kill me too.

I texted, 'Hey sorry if this is triggering. Are you okay?'

'Yes, it's triggering. I haven't slept yet and I'm about to go into a job so I guess we'll just leave it off here.'

We left it there until the jury reached its verdict. I asked her if it was okay to publish our email exchange. She replied:

> Knock yourself out, so long as you make it abundantly clear that he groomed me, and then obtained the relationship by deception. I'm a victim of extraordinary domestic abuse.
>
> It's also important for me to highlight that the Crown asserted that my ability to have a loving relationship was questionable because of my occupation. It's outdated and misogynistic and quite frankly with no basis in fact. They had three weeks of phone intercept listening to me as a loving partner who would've paid her fair share of a mortgage equally as well as all the bills. I am absolutely and have always been capable of a mutual respectful loving relationship, unfortunately on the same level of Pauline.

> Philip had it all, hot wife, he had a hot de facto girlfriend, he could have bookings for days with sex workers to blow some steam. And yet he still fucked it up which says a whole lot more about men than it ever will about women.

It was weird to receive these psychological commentaries during the trial. They were coming from the other side of the world (she celebrated her fiftieth birthday in Sicily) but they felt like messages from the Other Side. Her absence gave her supernatural powers; she had become a ghost, haunting courtroom 11, searched for but never found, spoken about but never seen. And all the while there she was yapping away in my inbox.

The secret knowledge of Madison's whereabouts operated as a fuel. I needed it to keep functioning. You could sense a fatigue in courtroom 11 as the weeks wore on; we were all being held captive, prisoners of a tragedy. The challenge was to emulate Ron Mansfield and stay trial fit. I measured my stamina in packed lunches; on Day 1 of the trial, I filled sandwiches with Moroccan fish stew made from Bill Granger's famous recipe, but by Week 6 I was throwing in a half-eaten, left-over hotdog. Every morning, I filled a thermos of Robert Harris Colombian Blend, the champagne of instant coffee. Every morning, I caught the 101 bus at 9.11 a.m. in my 1011 postcode and every morning I ran late but never once missed it. Every morning, I got off at the university bus stop and drifted to court through the lovely campus gardens, swooning at the arboretum of exotic trees: the tree rhododendron from the Himalayas, the windmill pine from Japan. One morning I took a small branch from the cowtail pine (also known as the Japanese plum tree) and laid it on the press bench at court. It looked like a fossil. I knew the feeling. The world had stopped spinning. Courtroom 11 was its frozen core. We had been sitting there, ancient and immobile, since the trial began 4.4 billion years ago when the Earth started cooling. All we knew was the Polkinghorne trial. We had checked into its Hotel California. An expert witness was called to describe the neurological experience of taking methamphetamine; she said it stimulated a profound release of dopamine into the synapse, i.e. it produced fabulous amounts of pleasure and it felt like the entire nation was smoking the Polkinghorne trial through the glass pipe of media coverage and getting shitfaced, really high, intensely happy — it gave New Zealanders so much excitement and pleasure. Yes, how terrible that it turned into a kind of carnival but there was a deep and profound sympathy for Pauline. She was always at the centre of courtroom 11. We gathered around her day and night. The trial took over our lives. I was eating it and sleeping it. One night I dreamed about it: Alysha McClintock had been replaced by Tiffany Cooper, a beautiful criminal defence lawyer in Auckland, and Brian Dickey had grown a long beard and hair past his shoulders. He said to me one day that he followed the court tradition of not cutting his hair during a trial, and my dream took him literally. There were a lot of people in dream court. I recognised the nice lady from Howick, the nice man from Northcote, and another woman who regularly attended the trial, but I never found out where she was from. It might have been Mars. She said to me one day, 'Have you noticed the parallels between Pauline's death and the death of Marilyn Monroe?' I said: 'No.' She said: 'There are many. Mark my words!' She was in the public gallery in my dream, leaving the courtroom. It had finished. A verdict had been reached. I felt devastated that it was all over.

---

Brian Dickey — the real one, fairly hirsute but without the ZZ Top dream beard — assumed an air of supreme indifference when I asked him how he felt about Madison's no-show. It was not the most convincing air I have ever seen. He shrugged a shoulder into this thin unconvincing air and was all very *qué será, será* about having to cope without his star witness in the trial of the century. 'We've got all her texts,' he said. 'So.'

The texts — and videos — were part of the stockpile gathered and read out in court by Detective Andrew Reeves. Their central value was that they established the close relationship between Madison and Polkinghorne. Goes to motive, etc. And it was evident that Polkinghorne's messages to her in the days following Pauline's death were not exactly the recommended textbook on how to mourn. They were Polkinghorne in heat, mad for it, the prolific author of wants and needs — another author puts it nicely: 'The expense of spirit in a waste of shame/ Is lust in action.' Shakespeare and Polkinghorne, together at last. My thanks to C.K. Stead, one of our greatest living authors, who responded to one of my *Herald* trial diaries by sending me the lines from Sonnet 129. They can be read as a comment that sex sometimes comes at a terrible cost, that it deranges the mind. Certainly sex distracts the mind. Death is too terrible, so sex is where we let ourselves feel. Or in the context of the trial, those lines can be read as Polkinghorne really not giving a fuck about Pauline's death and having better things to occupy his mind. Polkinghorne, messaging Ashton in response to photos she sent of her cosmetic surgery: 'Breasts bulging in perfect unison waiting to be unleashed to my tongue and fingertips. Omg the experience will be heavenly!' And: 'For your business it will I bet drive a tsunami of lust and will monetise your body further!' Also: 'For me I get to fuck you endlessly!'

At 4 p.m. on the Easter Monday of Pauline's death, Madison sent him a link to an image of herself in a swimsuit, making slow-cooked lamb shanks for her chihuahuas Brock, Daddy and Chanel. There were intercepted messages revealing they were looking at real estate listings in Sydney's Millers Point ('A historic enclave with nineteenth-century terraced houses and Harbour Bridge views'). There were twelve videos of Madison nude or *déshabillée*. Polkinghorne: 'How can you be so stunning?' There was quite a lot of to-ing and fro-ing to arrange their rendezvous in Mount Cook. Madison: 'Is it posh?' He assured her it was. The room with views of the Ben Ohau Range cost $2985. Madison: 'I love the fact that rural New Zealand isn't bursting with critters and things that can kill you.' She might have been wrong about that.

'Darling,' writes Polkinghorne, 'we are going to last 100 years.' He had recently turned 68. There is an insincerity about the few times Polkinghorne expresses something other than wanting to fuck Madison. The statements read as over the top, performative. He seems his true self only when the subject is sex. 'Oh goodness something has happened to me,' he salivates, in thrall to his own body, responding to yet another of Madison's nudes. Their dialogue often reads like a couple talking past each other, pursuing their own idea of themselves. Madison chats about buying 'anti-barking' collars for 'my children', meaning her chihuahuas; Polkinghorne turns the subject back to himself, and asks if she had bought him a collar, too. Eight days after Pauline's death, they discuss living together, and Ashton suggests they 'come up with house duties who does what'. Polkinghorne replies, grandly, 'I am good at ironing and grocery shopping and putting the rubbish out and can cook I can water plants and wash dogs and freeze bananas.' Let the record state that Polkinghorne can freeze bananas. But just like his cold, ChatGPT-esque message to Pauline when he was wanting to end his marriage, he types out a kind of HR warning to Madison that there may be difficulties: 'I think we should just see how it goes with no big ambition. If we gel great, but if it is too hard well that's life. I am really dying to see you all the same and just talk. I am not going to change your life or attempt too [sic] and whilst I have plans for the future I am sure you do too, there maybe commonality or maybe not. I have missed having dinner with you and talking as much but that's all I want to say.'

Madison: 'Okay sounds like you're breaking up with me.'

Polkinghorne: 'Fuck no! Christ no. I haven't come this far to walk away.'

Tempting to read something sinister in the 'I haven't come this far', and wonder exactly what he meant by 'this'. According to Madison, he lied to her about Pauline's suicide. She told *Stuff* journalist Paula Penfold, 'He was quite distressed, crying, and took him a little while to actually tell me what had happened to Pauline . . . He said she had come back to the house and committed suicide in order to punish him.' Pauline, she claimed he said, had 'let herself into the house somehow, without triggering the alarm'. Polkinghorne, busy as ever, busily altering the facts, busily wanting to keep Madison sweet. He was always in movement, in perpetual motion, a shark that would die if it stayed still — you can picture Polkinghorne in cartoon form, always in a rush, his body propelled by speed lines. But he looks perfectly content and very relaxed in a series of photographs that Madison took of him when they were together. There he is, his shirt off, in the kitchen; there he is, in Santa hat, at the Christmas he told Pauline he had to attend a counselling session. He looks peaceful. He looks calm. He was killing time his favourite way; all the photos have a cartoon quality, too: imagine not speed lines, but wavy lines indicating a scent is rising from his body. He looks like he smells of sex. They had a very good professional relationship. The problem was making it something else, something intimate. Madison gave him her heart. 'Honestly I really love you,' she messaged him. Another text read, 'I love you and I'll be true always.' She admired his intelligence, his dry wit, his generosity. She was loyal to him after Pauline died. The court heard she stood by him. Mansfield, in his cross-examination of Detective Reeves: 'He became isolated and the only person who provided support outside of his family and communicating regularly with him was Ms Ashton?' Reeves, who kept a log of phone intercepts, said this was correct. But any future together was built on and around Polkinghorne's lies: that he and Pauline had separated years previously, that she somehow got into the house to die by suicide as a form of punishment. After Madison found out the truth, she cut off all ties. She only ever used plain language, direct and to the point; she told Paula Penfold, 'This person to me now has become a dickhead.'

In the emails we exchanged, and the Polkinghorne comms that the police intercepted, there was a strong sense of her as someone who valued her independence above everything, held to a righteous belief that she knew right from wrong, truth from lies, black from white. She accused Polkinghorne of narcissism but she also sometimes came across as a raving narcissist herself. I sympathised with the police: it was easy to imagine her wanting to appear in the witness box to make it all about her. Her probative value was to establish the deep bond Polkinghorne felt for her, and to talk about his methamphetamine use. Beyond that, who cared? The Crown might only have led evidence in chief from her for about an hour.

On her website, she claims younger sex workers look up to her as an icon, and takes credit for popularising two kinds of sex work — PSE (porn star experience) and GFE (girlfriend experience) — in Australia: 'I single handedly launched two big, shiny, dazzling sex services that officially put the term PSE and GFE on the map. This terminology has become the industry norm. But just so you know dearies, it is mine. I broke it in. I developed it. I *perfected* it in this country', etc. She is open about her sex work, proud of her expertise; much of her site reads like a master plumber in supreme command of that trade, which like her own line of work is centred on liquid indignities. On cosmetic surgery:

> One of the procedures I had done is a lip lift: the shortening of the philtrum, the little line from the peak of your lip to the bottom of your nostril. When they shorten this gap under your nose, it brings your lip up, creating a prettier, more youthful effect. To do it, the filler had to come out first. Post-op, as soon as my new (and weirdly natural) lips encountered their first cock, I didn't get the right pressure on the shaft, with that

> snugness and powerful feeling of suction that makes for an epic blowjob.

Her services include anal sex; she narrates in third person, 'Madison prepares her body in a Zen-like state prior to your enjoyment.' SBS Australia filmed a twelve-minute story of her life, *The Making of Madison Ashton*, in 2016. She is shown selecting strap-ons and recommending lubricants. The programme also revealed that her mother was bipolar and died by suicide. And that she was introduced to sex work at fourteen. And that she has a close bond with her teenage daughter, but to Carolyne Meng-Yee in 2024 she described her relationship with both her children as 'estranged'.

Everything is drama, chaos, capitalism. She went to court as cardboard billionaire Richard Pratt's former mistress, to claim a promised $500,000 share of his estate; the judge recognised such a conversation did happen, but that Pratt had no intention of it being legally binding. She lost the claim. She told Carolyne Meng-Yee that Polkinghorne gave her hundreds of thousands of dollars over the years, including paying for her Sydney apartment and a six-figure sum for her legal fees in a trademark dispute. They had virtual dinners twice a week. He would make a table setting for her. They stayed in touch with daily texts, and video chats from his bed. 'He would come over to Sydney every month or so,' she told police — before that relationship, too, ended badly.

You wonder whether she and Polkinghorne would have ever had a chance of making things work, of finding happiness together. His trial was as much about their love story as the love story between him and Pauline. For all the playful texts, the promise of frozen bananas, the declarations of love, and recognising that they had taken it well beyond a professional arrangement into something personal and meaningful (he met her kids, she showed him where she grew up), there was something combustive and grotesque about the two of them. Their intercepted texts included an argument when Polkinghorne was due to meet her in Sydney for Christmas, but cancelled when he got the wrong idea she had a booking for sex work. 'If you want to work during the time I am in Sydney I should cancel my trip,' he wrote, once more in HR mode, or in the language of her employer. She replied, 'Thank you so much for fucking ruining Xmas. Fuck off. I am just so unbelievably devastated that you think so lowly of me and that you would think I would do that. Just says where your head is at not mine. I have no bookings.' She added, 'You have a gutter mentality when it comes to me and my occupation.'

One of my prized literary possessions is a signed copy of *In the Freud Archives*, Janet Malcolm's classic 1984 study of a relationship gone horribly wrong between two psychoanalysts. The signature is from one of the psychoanalysts, Jeffrey Masson, who left the US in disgrace after the book was published and fished up in Auckland. We got to know each other, and I loved his company, his intelligence, his excitability. He was immortalised as the book's villain, and he signed my copy with the inscription, 'Who is this guy? Not me! But you get it which is why we get on so well.' Actually, I never disputed Malcolm's portrait of Masson. It sounded exactly like the reckless and charming guy I knew. The book examined the way Masson and Kurt Eissler were drawn to each other. Malcolm writes, 'That things should have ended so badly between them was probably inevitable.'

I thought it was just as true of Madison and Polkinghorne: the inevitability of two like-minded, impulsive souls ending in disaster. I was worried that it would also be true of me and Madison. We stayed in touch after the verdict, and when she said she was coming to Auckland, I scheduled a lunch at the Park Hyatt.

CHAPTER 7

# 'I'm worried some things will come out'

Without Madison Ashton, the Crown case lawyers chuntered on, tossing and turning, leering and jeering, full of hints and innuendos, grasping at a great many straws and hurriedly strapping them together into a raft which they tried their hardest to row to shore — I was reminded of their efforts a week after the verdict when I read *Guardian* football writer Barney Ronay came up with a much better metaphor of something that was barely able to stay afloat. He filed a match report of England playing very badly and very haphazardly under an interim manager: 'It was like watching someone trying to construct a dinghy out of only liquorice, diamonds and vibes. At some point you will need some twine and a bit of driftwood. But carry on. It's kind of mesmerising.' Both the Crown and England lost, but not without sparkle, with razz if not full-on matazz, their respective vessels (the raft made of straws, the liquorice dinghy) going down like the *Titanic*.

As the weeks wore on, the immensity and grandeur of the Crown's leaking tub continued to make for mesmerising viewing. The peasants continued to pour into courtroom 11. But the High Court had enough of the ferals, of their crowding at the front door. Security guards were unable to hold them back. Lawyers had to shoulder barge through them to get in. It didn't bother me — they parted like the Red Sea whenever I approached. 'Steve!' One day I arrived to find that a clever new measure had been introduced to enforce crowd control. Security brought in a velvet rope. They positioned it about 5 metres from the front door. It was a flimsy little thing and I nursed revolutionary hopes that the mob would rise up against this bossy totalitarian attempt at segregation, use it to ram through the front doors, and stampede inside to take their rightful place in the arena of open justice. But the New Zealand mind is obedient. We never saw a velvet rope that we didn't meekly stand and wait behind. We, the sheeple.

At the first sight of the velvet rope, the flock set up an angry baaing; but no one dared touch it. The consequences were dire. They were addressed by the one female guard on security detail, a woman with short blonde hair and an unsmiling demeanour. She told them that any sign of rebellion, any attempt to cross the line drawn in the sand by a velvet rope, would mean instant dismissal from the High Court precinct. The threat of expulsion and trespass hung in the air like a dreadful sword. The guard raised her voice and said: 'This is a lawful direction!' That shut them up. But they rallied and soon regained their humour. Good on them. Open justice is an important principle. It's inclusive, it educates. A Year 11 schoolboy from Kristin School in the North Shore attended the trial in its last few weeks. 'I have started the Law Mooting Club at school,' he explained.

They came for the sex, the drugs, the rock'n'roll — there was a reference to Polkinghorne and Pauline going to Spark Arena to watch Crowded House in concert, so in fact not very rock'n'roll at all. But there was something else operating beyond the tabloid revelations, the rutting, the ruling class gone mad. For much of the trial a kind of vapour, something miasmic, hung low over the courtroom. I dwelled on this sense one weekend riding the bus to Papatoetoe to pick up an angel wing begonia I bought on TradeMe — houseplants were my relaxant during the trial, my escape. It was a cold day and grey clouds blanked out the sky. The low-roofed homes of brick and stucco squatted on small sections with old bombs parked on the front lawn and signs advertising Chinese medicine, hair braiding, Thai massage. My thoughts were never far from the trial — the happy sight of the angel wing begonia left in a paper bag by the front door of a middle unit offered a moment's escape — and the immigrant housing reminded me of the word that described that miasma in courtroom 11. In the original Arabic, ةلهو. In later, contemporary use in parts of Africa, *wahala*. In English, anxiety. The anxiety and terror of Pauline's death, as outlined by the Crown: *wahala*. The anxiety and terror of her hanging, as proposed by the defence: *wahala*. The terror of whatever happened that night to leave Pauline dead: *wahala*. It drifted like fog through the proceedings, touched every surface, lingered long after you left court each day.

Each afternoon I walked back through the university campus — once again admiring the kawaka tree with its bark torn to shreds, and the flaming reds of the firewheel tree, which gave the grounds their only colour that winter — to catch the 101 bus back home, and I'd start writing the day's *Herald* diary on my phone. I had to write fast before the phone died; I was continually pressing SAVE DRAFT as the power ran down to 10 per cent power, to five, to one; but that never bothered me very much, I loved the idea that journalism is literature in a hurry. Another, separate concern hovered over the little fading screen. A woman had died. The circumstances — murder, or suicide — were terrible. I thought of the Hanna family sitting directly behind me in court, all of them wearing White Ribbon pins condemning violence against women. I thought of the bright orange rope hanging from the balustrade. I thought of Polkinghorne carrying a human cargo as he came down the stairs with an intention to locate that rope, that belt. I thought of the royal spoonbills, white-faced herons and pied stilts bending their heads low to feed on the tide at Ōrākei Basin beneath the Polkinghorne home. I thought of Pauline looking forward to her upcoming 4WD holiday driving through the Middle Earth majesties of Central Otago. I thought of Polkinghorne staring at porn on the last night of her life. I thought of the police photos taken the next morning of bananas rotting in the fruit bowl, of three slices of bread placed in the toaster, of the three full cat bowls on the floor next to Pauline's body. All of it, ةلهو; all of it, *wahala*.

---

The trial spectators came for the drugs. They got a lot of drugs. There were two genres: illegal (the 37.7-gram stash of methamphetamine at the Polkinghorne home, enough for 370 hits of this white powder of madness) and legal (Pauline's not insubstantial stash of antidepressants). The two genres were a kind of his and hers pharmacology. Each played a crucial role, argued the two sets of lawyers, in Pauline's death.

The antidepressants prescribed to Pauline were known in ancient sexist times (the 1960s) as mother's little helpers. In answer to defence lawyer Hannah Stuart's long cross-examination, Pauline's doctor stiffly denied her patient was zonked on Prozac (67 scripts), weight-loss med Duromine (55 scripts), the sleeping medication zopiclone (she was taking it for at least six months), as well as alcohol suppressant naltrexone, and some appetite suppressants. Pauline, the doctor said, was coping perfectly well on weight-loss med Duromine (55 scripts), the sleeping medication zopiclone (she was taking it for at least six months), Prozac (she was taking it for about twenty years), as well as alcohol suppressant naltrexone, and the appetite suppressants. The quack acknowledged it looked bad on paper but said that real life was different. Yes, said the GP, Pauline could be characterised as having 'chronic depression'. The fact that she was on Prozac for twenty years suggested it was doing what it was intended for, said the Hippocratic oather who clung to name suppression . . . A number of witnesses made you wish you could benefit from their services. Polkinghorne's personal trainer, Barry Payne, inspired confidence with his enthusiasm and commitment. Polkinghorne's investment advisor, Tony Glucina, presented like a walking get-rich scheme.

Forensic scientist Helen Poulsen conducted Pauline's toxicology report. She found traces of zopiclone, fluoxetine (an antidepressant) and phentermine (a diet drug) alongside alcohol in her blood. The quantity of zopiclone was about two times higher than the recommended dose for therapeutic use, she said. 'In addition, patients taking zopiclone should be warned not to take alcohol at the same time. Using alcohol with sedatives tends to accentuate the effects of sedatives, and it is potentially quite dangerous to mix alcohol and sedative drugs like zopiclone.' Pauline sank a bottle of wine most nights for the past ten years.

Pauline's doctor took a less cautionary view in her cross-examination. Hannah Stuart asked if there are dangers of mixing alcohol and antidepressants. 'Yes, on paper,' said the doctor, appearing in court on a powerful name suppressant. 'In real life, it can go together. If you knew Pauline Hanna, you wouldn't say that. I guess I don't know how many of you have seen Pauline Hanna sitting in front of them and presenting the way she was.'

Pauline's best friend Pheasant Riordan was in court that day, as she often was during the trial; she knew Pauline probably better than just about anyone, including Polkinghorne, and she held no concerns about the way Pauline was handling her life. Mansfield asked if she was aware Pauline was on antidepressants. She replied, 'Who isn't?' It was the best zinger of the entire trial. Laughter brought the courtroom to a better place. Pheasant's comic timing was perfect, and it introduced a common sense to the issue: taking antidepressants was no big deal. Her meds and her drinking never struck Pauline's friends and colleagues as something that had got out of hand. Former Auckland District Health Board chief executive Ailsa Claire said in court, 'She was thriving.' Sarah Prentice worked with Pauline during the Covid vaccination roll-out, and said in the witness box, 'I didn't notice any particular stress.'

But two expert witnesses called by the defence issued grave warnings about Pauline's dependency. Sydney-based psychiatrist Dr Olav Nielssen singled out zopiclone sleeping pills; when combined with chronic depression and alcohol, he said they can be 'very dangerous for suicide'. Then he singled out the weight-loss drug phentermine as potentially having the greatest impact: 'It's got a whole bunch of worrying side effects, foremost of which is depression.' Raglan-based psychiatrist David Menkes mooched in wearing what looked like a velvet smoking jacket. He had the louche bohemian manner associated with that seaside town. Menkes also singled out phentermine and zopiclone. 'They keep people awake and they can produce a degree of mood instability,' he said of the former; as for the sleeping pill, it reacts strongly with alcohol and can both worsen depression and increase disinhibition, resulting in 'a considerable risk of harm'.

---

Just as Pauline's antidepressants were seen by prosecution as helping to stabilise her mood, and by defence as sending her into a spiral of unhappiness, Polkinghorne's drug of choice was viewed by prosecution with dark foreboding and by defence as a fun thing to do to help pass the time between cradle and grave. Methamphetamine was the only thing that Polkinghorne got done for. His guilty plea on Day 1 of the trial was like a white flag of surrender. He would not argue over whether he had it or smoked it. Ron Mansfield ran with the line that Polkinghorne's taste for methamphetamine was a kind of hobby, another of his harmless recreations alongside sex workers. It was a party drug. It was a sex drug.

But methamphetamine is not MDMA, not some variant of Viagra. Methamphetamine will fuck you up. We demonise methamphetamine as the leading cause of terror in twenty-first-century New Zealand life, a white *wahala*, because it actually is the ruin of communities and the source of wealth for its distributors, including the violent, heavily armed 501 deportee gang Comancheros. The fact that a Remuera ophthalmologist had it in the first place, and in such quantities, was so jarring, so incongruous. But that was Polkinghorne. He was Superman in the supermarkets of sex and drugs. He bought what he wanted. He did things his way, searching Google on how to make a glass pipe out of a lightbulb to smoke P ('Take a 60-watt bulb and break off the black stuff on the bottom with a flathead screwdriver', advised some crackhead). He defied convention. He sat back in his white, bland house ('Meticulously manicured gardens set a scene of peaceful tranquillity', raved its real estate advertisements), and stoked up the glass barbecue all that good, good.

There was an interesting cameo of Polkinghorne introducing the subject of methamphetamine in a gracious Remuera setting.

It went down badly. A friend and former colleague at Auckland Eye, surgeon Susan Ormonde, was called as a witness. They formed a great team on the fields of opthamology. 'Philip dealt with the back of the eye,' she said, 'and I deal with the front of the eye.' She was asked about inviting Polkinghorne to her house for lunch the day before Pauline's funeral. Ormonde had long, grey hair with a middle parting and a straightforward manner; easy to imagine her frozen expression when their lunch took an unexpected turn. She relayed their dialogue in court.

Polkinghorne said to her, 'I'm worried some things will come out.'

She asked, 'What things?'

'Mine and Pauline's sex life,' he said, 'and drugs.'

She asked, 'What drugs?'

'Meth,' he said. 'Have you tried it?'

'No,' she replied.

He said, 'You should.'

Interesting lunch! Afterwards, Polkinghorne made a voluntary disclosure to the Medical Council about his meth use. Other colleagues from Auckland Eye were also called as witnesses; their probative value was to share their concerns about Polkinghorne's erratic conduct at work, his mood swings, his strangeness. The insinuation was that methamphetamine will and does make you crazy. Board chair Mark Connelly spoke of Polkinghorne's behaviour at a Zoom meeting: 'He was very agitated — in fact, outright rude to the staff. Everyone was looking sideways, like, "What's going on here?" He was quite intimidating. I said to him, "You can't behave like that."'

Auckland Eye's former CEO Deborah Boyd gave evidence that Polkinghorne appeared to fall asleep at a March 2021 finance committee meeting. She spoke in a small, uncertain voice. The only thing upfront about her was a large pair of black-rimmed glasses. 'His eyes,' she quavered, 'were shut.' Ron Mansfield established in his very long cross-examination that the meeting was held in the offices of an accountancy firm on a Friday, that the weather that day was unseasonably warm, and much on the agenda that day was of little importance . . . The long, boring, stiflingly hot day cooped up in an accountancy firm was so realistically evoked in Mansfield's cross-examination that it felt like the meeting was still taking place, but it had moved to courtroom 11 at the High Court of Auckland. Falling asleep at a finance committee meeting is not a criminal offence. It is inevitable, almost mandatory.

There were other times when the Crown seemed to be getting nowhere with the meth evidence, or when they were being led into a brick wall by Mansfield. A health professional with name suppression talked about the fantastical delicacies of the retina, and the surgical precision that was required. 'The retina itself is only a matter of microns thick. It has to be treated with the utmost care.' To which prosecutor Brian Dickey burst in, and said, 'Would you describe it as irresponsible and reckless to be taking methamphetamine as an eye surgeon?' The mind, or something, boggled at the prospect of a P fiend taking a scalpel to the vulnerable microns of the retina. The witness replied, 'Certainly if you were operating it would.' But there was no evidence that Polkinghorne performed surgery while skating on the thin ice of methamphetamine.

And then there was the saga of high levels of methamphetamine detected at Auckland Eye. It began when Auckland Eye's clinical services manager Janet Wigmore was 'showing the ropes' to two staff members on a Monday morning in October 2020, walked into the retinal laser room, and saw a glass methamphetamine pipe and lighter on a table. 'I backtracked and closed the door,' she said. The comedy of it — oh, let's not go in this room! — continued when she alerted CEO Deborah Boyd. Boyd engaged law firm Wynn Williams (situated way up high on the twenty-fifth floor of the Vero Centre skyscraper on Shortland Street) to investigate. It led to a drug-testing technician, Jeremy Hill, arriving at Auckland Eye late one night in an unmarked car. Boyd was waiting for him. *Good evening!* 'We weren't able to turn up there with branded vans so used a non-marked car and I wasn't wearing any signage, to keep it confidential,' he said in the witness box. Under cloak of darkness, Hill took fourteen samples from four rooms. A swab from the heat pump grill in consult room 4 returned a high level of methamphetamine. He recommended that Auckland Eye engage the services of a reputable cleaning company to decontaminate.

Such discretion, such subterfuge; reputational damage control is such an interesting field of work. But what did the methamphetamine discovery have to do with Polkinghorne? One proven method to create reasonable doubt is to complicate things more than is necessary. Mansfield decided to take a great interest in the mysterious workings of internal and external heat pumps. How, he pondered, did the traces of methamphetamine arrive on the surface of the heat pump grill in consult room 4? Could they have travelled from outside? You pictured Mansfield squeezing through the aircon ducts in Auckland Eye, torch in hand, in the manner of Bruce Willis stripped down to his singlet and crawling through the ventilation tunnels as John McClane in *Die Hard*.

His cross-examination of Jeremy Hill, the drug-testing tech, was delivered in classic Mansfield style: with narrowed eyes, gritted teeth.

'Did you go outside and test the exterior units for contamination?'

'No.'

'Can you even tell us where the exterior units were?'

'No.'

It wasn't exactly the *Die Hard* riposte of 'Yippee-ki-yay, motherfucker' but it allowed for the remote possibility that someone other than Polkinghorne had introduced methamphetamine traces into Auckland Eye and you take every little partial or barely formed victory you can in a murder trial.

---

There was another, equally involving narrative to the parade of Auckland Eye employees who appeared as witnesses for the Crown. They were there to say things about methamphetamine but ended up saying things about the place where they worked. In essence they described Auckland Eye in 2019 as a total shitshow. The board, said chair Mark Connelly, was 'battered and bruised' that year after two shareholders departed in 'controversial, sudden and unexpected' circumstances. After litigation they each eventually received payouts of $650,000. Other shareholders felt betrayed, he said. Polkinghorne felt betrayed, too, and increasingly bitter. He was nearing retirement and agitating for his own handsome payout. The inner workings of it were revealed in cross-examination.

Mansfield asked Connelly to confirm that the two specialists who left Auckland Eye were paid $650,000 upon their acrimonious departure in 2019, plus interest.

Connelly said that was subject to a confidentiality agreement.

Mansfield asked if his figures were wrong.

Connelly said they were not wrong.

Mansfield asked if Polkinghorne was offered $360,000.

Connelly said that was about right.

Polkinghorne eventually received $450,000, but he still felt short-changed, bilked, ripped-off. Connelly said the payout was discussed at a March 2020 Zoom call. He had told Polkinghorne his payout was in line with the shareholder agreements, including the fact it took into account the sale of property and dividends already paid. Polkinghorne replied that he wasn't happy and made it clear that, at a minimum, he wanted at least what the two doctors who left in 2019 had got.

But this was a murder trial, not an employment tribunal; what was the relevance? To Mansfield, all of it — the dispute, the insulting payout, the hurt and anger that Polkinghorne felt — went towards explaining the mood swings and general state of anxiety that his client presented in the years before Pauline's death. His argument was supported by a reliable witness: Pauline. She wrote in October 2020, 'I just CAN'T WAIT to get him out of there!!! It is insanely wrong to treat him like this and he is taking it all so personally . . . He has had so many blows from them. Last night he said, "They all hate me, this is aimed at me, why are they doing this to me?"

He is devastated and gutted that after 30 years he is in this position . . . He is quite distraught and this is awful for the person who started the business and being treated so badly.' She gossiped about a board member who had to resign after it was revealed he had an affair with a charge nurse at Auckland Eye, and I remembered Deborah Boyd's small, pointed face and shy manner when Pauline described the former CEO as 'worse than useless'. All of it — the litigation, the bitterness, the affair, the bottom line — was a reminder that there is something far more damaging and injurious to our long-term mental health than methamphetamine: the office.

---

As much as Ron Mansfield tried to wave away the meth smoke, its weird sharp whiff clung to Polkinghorne from the moment he pleaded guilty to possession of the stash and the pipe. He owned it, literally. After the verdict, Madison Ashton talked with real fondness of Polkinghorne smoking the drug and turning into a dancing queen, and there was a photo of her lying naked on her front next to her dogs and the dear old SWEET PUFF meth pipe. She spoke, too, of her concern that it was causing him to shed weight and look emaciated ('His skin was limp on his backside.') A colleague at Auckland Eye who gave evidence at the trial was likewise startled at his rapid weight loss to the point where she worried that Polkinghorne might have cancer.

So he smoked it. So its aphrodisiacal qualities were appealing. So it can stimulate up to 1200 units in the pleasure treasuries of dopamine, compared to a mere 300 stimulated by cocaine, as drug expert Dr Emma Schwarcz advertised its power in the witness box. So what, except that the Crown was hardly drawing on a long bow to connect P use to violence. 'There's a positive association between aggression and methamphetamine use across the range of studies,' Schwarcz confirmed. She also said that prolonged use can lead to agitated states of behaviour, and this was illustrated by the Crown's most convincing witness in its methamphetamine narrative.

Ship's master Stephen MacIntyre was called early on in the trial. He testified via audio-video feed from the High Court of Wellington. He was lavishly moustachioed and came across like a straight shooter, i.e. exactly the kind of person who Mansfield never gets very far with in cross-examination.

He had once been close friends with Polkinghorne. They summered together with their wives for about 25 years at the beautiful Rings Beach on the Coromandel Peninsula. The two men went fishing, diving, swimming. All the classic New Zealand summers enjoyed by the bach-owning class.

But his neighbour started to change, MacIntyre said at the trial. Like Madison Ashton, and like Polkinghorne's colleague at Auckland Eye, he thought Polkinghorne had lost a lot of weight. He also thought he acted differently: 'He was manic and irrational at times. I certainly considered that he was in a mind-altered state on several of those occasions.'

Crown prosecutor Brian Dickey: 'What do you mean by that?'

MacIntyre: 'I thought he was using drugs.'

I performed a disservice to MacIntyre when I wrote up that day in court for the *Herald*. I seized on a line of questioning from Ron Mansfield, when he said to him in cross-examination,

'You mentioned Dr Polkinghorne's "generosity". Well, you'll remember having an issue with your eyes, and calling him, leaving a message, and him calling you straight back, and he told you to get to Auckland immediately, and you were worried about his other patients, but he said he would clear the decks to see you.'

MacIntyre: 'Correct.'

Mansfield: 'So when you needed him, he was there for you.'

MacIntyre: 'Correct.'

But, said Mansfield, after news media reported the 'unexplained' death of Hanna, MacIntyre told police he had concerns about Polkinghorne's behaviour. Yes, replied MacIntyre, that was correct, too.

At the time I felt this was a poor show from Polkinghorne's seaside neighbour. I wrote that he seemed ungrateful, had turned on a friend who went to great lengths to help him out. The only problem was in my head; I have an abiding dislike of the social media pile-on, and I think I took it out on MacInytre, whom I saw as forgetting that Polkinghorne had done him a great favour, and I was a bit too willing to stick the knife in. But this was impetuous and stupid. MacIntyre was just saying it like he saw it. Equally, he was saying it out of concern.

He was asked to read out his police statement. The moustache parted and went up and down as he said the words. There is a unique formality to a police statement. It's an accurate statement — the speaker signs it — but it's not verbatim, it lacks the rhythm and patterns of speech and has a unique elliptical stiffness. Each sentence reads like a self-contained paragraph. And yet MacIntyre's statement was like a short story told in song. I heard it as a Johnny Cash ballad. The opening verses set the scene.

> I felt that Dr Polkinghorne was changed.
> Some things that I saw and felt I didn't particularly like.
> I probably just backed off the relationship a little bit.
> He was a very intelligent, funny, witty, generous man.
> We always had a lot of laughs together.

The next two lines read like a chorus.

> In that period leading up to Pauline's death, I felt that he was quite changed.
> His nature changed, his physical presence changed.

The next verse picks at the same scab, deepens it.

> He became slimmer and sort of more muscly.
> He became a bit more manic, a little bit irrational.
> I didn't think he was behaving normally
> or truthfully to me at all times.
> I felt he was using drugs.

The last line is the best line. It's as though the music stops. Silence surrounds MacIntyre as he leans into the microphone, the ship's master as grave as Johnny Cash, and speaks from the heart.

> I was trying to find an explanation as to why my friend was now acting like a weirdo.

In a case beset with contradictions and mysteries and guesswork and resemblances and suspicions and implications and shadows, it was a line that cut through to the core of things. In a case miserable in its lovelessness, it spoke of one person ('my friend') caring about another.

CHAPTER 8

# In Defence of Polkinghorne

The first witness in the opening day in the defence of Dr Philip Polkinghorne was, astonishingly, Pauline's younger sister, Tracey, who sided with Polkinghorne and claimed Pauline had tried to kill herself years previously, and had finally succeeded. It was a day that also saw Polkinghorne's family come to court for the first time in an impressive, unified show of love and support. It was not a day to be missed. Yet on the morning of that Friday of astonishments, I opened the hotel room curtains and gazed at the long snow-white line of the Southern Alps.

It was with a heavy heart that I missed the crucial opening day of Polkinghorne's defence to appear at the Christchurch Word literary festival. I sulked in my ninth-floor room of the Crowne Plaza in downtown Christchurch and joined everyone else in New Zealand who wanted a Polkinghorne fix by reading the live blog by the *Herald*'s indefatigable George Block. Eventually it was time to tear myself away from his instant record of history, and head to a stunning little theatrette on Armagh Street opposite The Seagull Pit, so-called for the colony of maybe 200 red-billed seagulls which have taken over the flooded foundations of an office block demolished after the 2011 earthquakes. I was interviewed onstage about a collection of true-crime essays, *The Survivors: Stories of Death and Desperation*. I enjoyed the session very much, not least because the first thing that event chair Philip Matthews asked, and the subject that everyone who queued up afterwards at the book signing wanted to talk about, was Polkinghorne, Polkinghorne, Polkinghorne. They were fascinated, dazzled, appalled; when I arrived in Christchurch, I wondered whether maybe the Polkinghorne trial was like a microclimate that only affected Auckland, the setting of the death, the scandal and the shopping. But the good people of Christchurch who I met after my event were just as glued to it as anyone in Auckland. It was just like being back in courtroom 11 except not really, not at all. I missed the place and rued that I wasn't there. I spent that weekend wandering alongside the slow-running waters of the Avon River and thinking back on the five weeks I had experienced within the box of the High Court of Auckland.

The last time I reported on a murder trial this long was way back in 2005 when Antonie Dixon set about achieving a rare paradox — he was an insane sonofabitch who attempted to impersonate an insane sonofabitch. He struck two women with a Samurai sword while smashed on methamphetamine. But that was simple compared with Polkinghorne. Dixon was poor white trash who had been tied to a clothesline and beaten as a kid. He did worse unto others. Polkinghorne was a skilled eye surgeon who made life immeasurably better for patients afraid of going blind, just another anonymous and blameless Merc-driving capitalist schnook until 5 April 2021, when he dialled 111 and said: 'My wife's dead. She hung herself.'

The waters of the Avon stroked the soft green riverbanks. I thought back to the Crown case, its five weeks of hopeful mayhem. It never seemed to truly get off the ground. It churned it into mud and got bogged down in it, particularly with the witnesses from Auckland Eye — which is now the most famous ophthalmology clinic in New Zealand but not really in a good way. Its doctors and executives seemed to be a horrible bunch and the workplace they described in 2019 felt toxic. It distracted from Polkinghorne's toxicity. There was some regret in the prosecution team after the trial about calling Auckland Eye staff to give evidence; it complicated things, was just another burden for the jury. It also left a sour taste.

Christchurch was smooth and silky in 19 degrees as sunlight gilded mountain snow. I thought back to some of the last witnesses and how little they contributed. There was the Polkinghorne housekeeper: the ever-gorgeous former queen of New Zealand pop music, Sheryl Morris, the most stylish witness of the entire trial in a crisp white shirt, its sharp collars over her black jacket, and her red hair piled high. Her most memorable contribution was to reveal that she cleaned the house four hours a day, twice a week. There was the very final witness, the most regal person to be called to the trial: Detective John Kennedy, since retired from the police, but very much active when his contribution to the case was enshrined as the cop who arrested Polkinghorne. He struck a marvellously patrician figure when he arrived in the witness box and preferred to stand, thank you, tall and gaunt in an olive sports jacket, his hands behind his back. Polkinghorne, that foul sex elf, looked up to the heavens at this fair cop. Kennedy told how he placed Polkinghorne under arrest at the College Hill police station at 7.55 a.m. on 16 August 2022. Significant moment: it brought to an end a police investigation that had crept along for sixteen months and eleven days, and all throughout the Crown's case you could sense the determination and also the frustration. Kennedy was one last brick in the wall, and it was a strange-looking wall, which is to say it often merely resembled a tonne of bricks dumped over the writhing figure of Polkinghorne in an attempt to bury any last shred of decency in his character. It was a pile-on, kind of crude, and sometimes the weight of evidence felt crushing and sometimes it felt irrelevant, and anyway it just kept coming.

Christchurch, or at least its downtown precinct, looks shinier, more restored, more interesting with every visit — it looks a hell of a lot better than downtown Auckland, that shambles of cones and wire fences, crews digging up the road, streets squeezed into one narrow lane, all of it looking like it's just been hit by an earthquake. Christchurch has moved on. I had not. I thought back to Ron Mansfield's cross-examination of another of the Crown's final witnesses, the head of Operation Kian, Detective Senior Sergeant Chris Allan. He sat in the witness box, chinless and clerical. Mansfield accused Allan and therefore the police of rushing to judgment and treating Pauline's death as suspicious. Allan said, 'We kept an open mind.'

Mansfield said, 'I wonder if we can just explore that open mind.'

He asked Allan about the decision to call in the then-Crown solicitor Brian Dickey to the Polkinghorne house during the forensic examination, which was after the discovery of the drugs. 'The Crown solicitor,' he asked, 'doesn't deal with possession of a methamphetamine pipe, correct?'

'Correct.'

'Only with an investigation of murder or manslaughter, correct?'

'Correct.'

'Police went to seventy-nine neighbouring properties, correct?'

'That's the routine, yes.'

'For a homicide inquiry, correct?'

'Yes,' said Allan, twitching.

Christchurch, I was told by a drinker in a downtown bar, was a missed opportunity to build the first great city of the twenty-first century, and that instead conservative minds rebuilt the last great city of the twentieth century. Interesting, but my mind was back in Auckland, as I read and re-read George Block's reporting of the evidence given by Tracey Hanna.

The day in court was like a family reunion gone wrong. Polkinghorne's three children appeared and so did their mother, Polkinghorne's first wife; her contribution was to confirm that her ex-husband hadn't strangled her to death. She made no eye contact with him in court, pretended he wasn't there: he wasn't in her life anymore, they had separated because he had an affair, she said in the witness box. As for Tracey Hanna: she made no eye contact with her family, either, gave no sign that her brother, Bruce Hanna, was in the court with his daughter and his son, Tracey's niece and nephew. Her contribution was to claim Pauline told her in around about 1992 that she had tried to die by suicide. It was after their father's death. She remembered going into the kitchen, where Pauline and their mother were having a dispute, both shouting and crying. 'Then she turned her anger onto me, and I can't remember, there was toing and froing and all of a sudden she [pause] she said that she'd tried to kill herself.' She further claimed she buried the memory for 32 long years, when Pauline's death, coming shortly after her mother's death in early 2021, made her think Pauline had once again reacted to a parent's death by wanting to take her own life, and this time had succeeded. All of which was news to the rest of her family. None of them had heard anything of the sort. In cross-examination, Brian Dickey asked her if the kitchen incident in 1992 (it might have been earlier, maybe 1990, she said) was the most dramatic event in her relationship with Pauline, and she answered, 'Until she actually killed herself.' Under pressure in cross-examination, she said to Dickey, 'You're making me feel very inadequate right now'; and when she was informed by the judge that she could leave the court, she said, 'Thank God.' Her family likely felt the same way to see the back of her.

Christchurch, with its own destiny, its own culture, even its own ophthalmology murder case (in 2023, Christchurch eye surgeon Ian William Dallison was sentenced to six years for the attempted murder of his former business landlord, shooting at him with a Ruger semi-automatic pistol while his victim was sitting down to dinner, the bullet narrowly missing his head and lodging itself in the doorframe over his right shoulder), was the same as I was: agog with Polkinghorne. Everyone in the book-signing queue after my session at The Piano bar raised it; and everyone had the same view. They included three people who were uncannily representative of the powers that be in the case of Philip John Polkinghorne. I spoke with a retired judge. 'I'd have found him guilty,' he said, 'but the jury won't.' I spoke with a retired police officer. 'Not enough against him,' he said, 'he'll get off.' I spoke with a retired pathologist. He had read the reports. Do they get shared around? Is there an email chain among Dr Deaths? I asked him what he thought. 'Not guilty,' he said, and turned and fled, a signed book clutched under his arm, when I asked him why. I was about to find out.

---

When I got back from Christchurch on the Monday of Week 6, the trial had shifted on its axis, and so, too, had the university clock tower which I greeted every morning on the way to the High Court. All throughout the Crown case, its hands were fixed at 12, signifying either the long shadows of high noon or the scarifying midnight hour, that portal to the underworld. It was as though the broken clock was mocking the gothic hues and cries of the prosecution. But now the clock had fixed itself at another time: 9. Again, it felt in sync with the Polkinghorne trial, and was showing the time as a commentary on the defence. I quickly divined that its weights and oscillations were working to read 9 a.m. as in the start of the working day, a wide-awake, reasonable, office hour, the hour of calmly presented available facts. The defence had come to straighten things out. It was above conspiracy theories, sex tapes, SWEET PUFF. The prosecution had crept around courtroom 11 for five weeks in its creepy midnight robes; the defence preferred the broad daylight of 9 a.m., and calmly went about presenting scientific fact. Polkinghorne had signalled this was going to happen. It happened, devastatingly.

One of the first things Polkinghorne said to me during the trial was after a day in court when his sex life was dragged in front of everyone. His face had gone red, he was fit to burst, he angrily put on his overcoat to head out into the cold winter evening, and said, 'You just wait for our science. That's what this is all about. The science. It's all in our science.' I said, 'What science?' He replied, 'Our pathology.'

He was right to look forward to it. It cleared the decks. It brought things back into focus. Not sex; not drugs; not the inconclusive science as collected at the Polkinghorne house between 8 a.m. and 8.30 p.m., etc., over 53 hours by the ESR. It called distinguished veteran pathologist Professor Stephen Cordner as its seventeenth witness. He was conclusive. He was adamant. Just as when I made a note of the exact date and time (Wednesday 13 August, 10.51 a.m.) that Crown pathologist Dr Kilak Kesha made the breathtaking revelation that he thought the belt was placed around Pauline's neck after she had died, I jotted down that it was precisely 10.57 a.m. on Friday 6 September, when — to the question of what he would have ruled as cause of Pauline's death — Cordner answered, 'I think I would have said cause of death was hanging, with no findings to support the alternative view of homicide. And — yeah. So.'

Yeah. So. So that was it, the jig was up. He put it another, more formal way: 'There is no evidence of a forensic pathology kind to positively support a conclusion that this deceased has been homicidally, manually or ligaturely killed.' Even in cross-examination he stuck to it, as inflexible as the hands of the university clock tower. He repeated it, sometimes verbatim, sometimes with minor variations, sometimes expanding on it. He perfected it at the very end of his evidence in chief, when Mansfield asked him, 'If you were responsible for this case, by way of being the attending pathologist, how would you have reported the cause of death?'

He replied, 'If I had been responsible for this case, I would have concluded the cause of death was hanging because the findings fit with hanging and there are no findings to support the alternative of homicidal ligature or manual strangulation.'

It felt like the trial, and the verdict, had reached the point of no return. The tent had collapsed. The stately ship had sunk. The sixteen months and eleven days of police work, the 60 witnesses called by the Crown — all of it, zero-sum. The case against Polkinghorne was over from that moment on, from 10.57 a.m., when Cordner — a pathologist who has held a position as professor of forensic medicine at Monash University, and with a long career in the mortuaries of the world — said there was no evidence that Pauline was killed.

He was believable, at the very least plausible. It helped that he was so personable. He was a Dr Death who looked like a kindly grandpa. Cordner was tall, thin, toothy, with red-rimmed glasses. He wore the same rumpled grey suit over two days in court. His head sported a big white cochlea implant drilled into the side of his skull. He spoke in a soothing voice, smiled often, self-effaced, laughed, seemed to regard the whole thing as a pleasant outing from his offices in Melbourne. He seemed like a man who enjoyed his work. Death was an intellectual puzzle; he had the experience to solve it. And yet he had a certain haplessness about him. I approached him one afternoon during a recess and asked about his cochlea. He leaned forward, and said, 'WHAT?' I repeated, loudly, 'HOW'S THAT COCHLEA WORKING OUT?' He leaned back, and said, 'Oh yes. Yes, very good. Very useful.' I said, 'I'm deaf as a post and have wondered about them, you see.' He said, 'WHAT?'

His evidence in chief began with absences, the missing things he would expect to see on Pauline's body had she been killed. 'We're looking for positive evidence of injury, we're looking for patterns of injuries, considerations of the injuries collectively. So the question here is, has the deceased been killed or did she kill herself? If she's been killed, then that means assault. So then are there injuries that are commonly associated with assault?' And so if she had been throttled with a belt, Pauline would likely have resisted, meaning the belt would have moved up and down against the neck, causing damage to the skin; but such damage was not found. As for the wounds that were present — a graze on the bridge of her nose, a small bruise on her temple — they were nowhere near the extent normally seen in strangulation victims. 'There's nothing incompatible in my view with the presence of those injuries and a conclusion of an incomplete hanging . . . The findings support hanging and there's no findings to support homicidal ligature or manual strangulation.'

He smiled throughout his evidence, a happy 71-year-old man who expressed himself with his long, beautiful hands — they were the fingers of death. They have touched so many bodies in death. The lovely hands clutched at his throat to imitate the crushing of the neck, to mime inflicting death. He said, 'The veins in the neck are thin walls. Very thin walls. They carry blood from the head to the heart, and the heart pumps it back up and takes oxygen to the head in an amazing circle of life.'

An amazing circle of life! He reminded me of Crown witness and drug expert Dr Emma Schwarcz, who was likewise awestruck at the speed and potency of methamphetamine. They approached their respective subjects with such pleasure, a joyousness.

Mansfield asked, 'How do you decide which is which, hanging or homicidal strangulation?' He replied, 'Yeah. Well. So. We look for signs, sort of like headlines, which allow us to distinguish the difference . . . The general accepted view is that homicidal strangulation is very often the endpoint of a sustained attack. So seventy per cent of these cases is that the person has been the victim of a much more sustained assault, and there would be bruises to the head or scalp, sometimes fractures, a general range of injuries.' He put it in even simpler terms: 'They've been beaten up.'

Pauline, he stated, did not have injuries commonly associated with assault. Her body was an absence. If she had been strangled, she would have put up some measure of resistance that would result in injuries. 'The assailant has to overcome the victim before the victim is in a position to be successfully strangled.' Mansfield asked about other absences, meaning the lack of drag marks on Pauline's body. Cordner replied, 'There might be abrasions on exposed skin that [has been] dragged across carpet or rough surfaces. You can get carpet burn.' Pauline did not have carpet burn.

The subject turned to the ligature marks around Pauline's neck which had completely disappeared the day after her death, and furthered the police theory it was a homicide. This was an absence that the police, and Dr Kesha, had seized on; Cordner expressed supreme indifference about it. 'To me, the disappearing mark has got no significance.' He has expressive shoulders as well as hands; he shrugged, and said, 'It is as it is. It's disappeared. It doesn't impress me one way or another as being worthy of suspicion.' He was reminded that the Crown's two pathologists thought it worthy of suspicion. He said, 'For some reason I don't understand, they think the disappearing marks are suspicious. But it's a well-recorded phenomenon.'

The furthest the Crown's two pathologists went was to say homicide and suicide were possible causes. Cordner: 'My view is that it's reasonable to go a bit further. The findings support hanging, and there's no findings to support homicide.'

Pauline's best friend Pheasant Riordan was in court that day. She wept hearing the graphic descriptions of death and had to leave. There was someone else who seemed overwhelmed by Cordner's account of blocking the arteries, which stops the flow of blood — breaking the circle of life — and causes death. Polkinghorne, 71, widower, sat in court with his hands pressed over his face, his eyes closed, in darkness, listening to the mechanics of Pauline's death.

On and on it went, the Crown tent collapsing all over courtroom 11, as Cordner held firm to the 9 a.m. of the mind and laid out his multitude of findings that did not support the theory that Pauline had been murdered. He was asked about the likelihood of Polkinghorne staging Pauline's death, by placing her body on a chair, tying a belt around her neck, and attaching the belt to a rope tied to an upstairs balustrade — all the evil little manipulations, the grotesque post-death conduct, of Polkinghorne creeping around the house, a tiny fellow with nasty little feet, choreographing an awful dance of death. But Cordner was having none of it. He was asked about the chances of Polkinghorne doing all those things. His answer: 'It's quite mind-boggling to imagine that, because that looseness and floppiness of the body makes the body very hard to manage.' Forensic pathologists, he said, held to a rule that it takes two people to manoeuvre a dead body.

Dr Death, avuncular, content, deaf as a post, had waved away the whole idea of Polkinghorne having the gall and the madness to carry Pauline's dead body down the stairs at some dismal hour after midnight, and prop it up on a chair in a gross mime of suicide. I had always struggled to imagine it. It wasn't that I didn't think he was capable of it. A murderer will go to any extreme to get away with it. But the awful tableau of it was weirdly more horrifying than the act of killing. The sheer nastiness of it was overwhelming. There was a terrible precedent: Jesse Kempson. That mad dog was found guilty of strangling Grace Millane to death, but what appalled even more, what sent it towards a cold depraved shore far from human decency, was what he did to dispose of her body. He bought a suitcase and stuffed her in it and buried it in the bush. The parallel with Polkinghorne was callous post-death conduct. Justice Simon Moore, when he sentenced Kempson, quoted from the nineteenth-century theologian Richard Bentley: 'Callousness does not require prolonged activity. It involves a lack of feeling, empathy and sensibility, once colourfully described as a "numbness of the soul".' Bentley prefaced that description by calling such killers 'destitute of common sense'. That was the portrait of Polkinghorne that the Crown wished to impress upon the court. Someone so destitute, his soul so numb, that he would string up his wife's dead body. But it didn't matter whether you could or could not imagine him performing such a dark foul deed with the body, the chair, the strips of leather and rope. Dr Death, in the rumpled, smiley shape of Professor Stephen Cordner, had no interest in whether Polkinghorne was morally capable of it; he simply stated that he was physically incapable of it. It never happened. To imagine it would be 'mind-boggling'.

After Cordner finished giving evidence, I asked Polkinghorne, 'Do you think the tide is turning?' He replied quickly, 'Oh, it's turned. It's already turned.'

---

There was another, more topical resonance of the 2021 Jesse Kempson murder trial during the 2024 Philip Polkinghorne murder trial. It went beyond the sickening parallels of post-death conduct, of the suitcase and the chair as ways and means to commit violence against women even after they had been killed. It was on TV. Halfway through the trial, Netflix started screening *The Lie: The Murder of Grace Millane*, a harrowing and expertly made documentary by British film-maker Helena Coan. Its long, slow, lingering drone shots above the Waitākere Ranges were like a wallpaper of horror. You did not see what happened; it was worse than that; you *felt* what happened: the repellent activities of Kempson digging a hole in the bush with a shovel to bury Grace inside a cheap suitcase. Much of the film was silent. There was no music or voice-over when it showed police photographs of where Kempson had fashioned the grave. There was the clearing in the bush. There was the patch of dirt. There was the suitcase.

It was not an exploitative film, but neither was it concerned with Kempson's defence — except to portray it as an outrageous abuse of power, particularly in its treatment of one witness, a victim of sexual violence, who came forward to tell the court Kempson had threatened to kill her. It played a segment of that cross-examination. It was awful to watch. It inspired hatred against the lawyer. The lawyer was Ron Mansfield.

I followed that trial and was there to observe that cross-examination. I felt it was Mansfield at his worst, a cold eyeless creature disguised behind his thick glasses, conducting himself without warmth or pity, with something resembling a numbness of the soul. As ever with Mansfield, he prolonged the agony; he never saw a cross-examination he didn't want to outstay its welcome. His cross-examination of the witness in the Kempson trial carried on for hours and hours and hours over a long, bad day in court and at 5 p.m. he said he needed to continue with it the next morning. The documentary, like the court itself during that trial, came close to loathing Mansfield more than his murderous client.

The timing of the release of *The Lie* was potentially damaging for Mansfield — I thought it made him look worse than bad — and, by association, for Polkinghorne. I had seen most of it already — the documentary made a lot of use of CCTV footage that was shown at the trial (Kempson meeting Grace outside Sky City on a Tinder date; Kempson and Grace getting drunk and hooking up; Kempson leaving his hotel two days later with a suitcase), and much was also taken from the trial itself. I feature in a live-action scene writing down notes in a 3B1 Warwick notebook. It was strange watching Mansfield in the film. He came across as so intensely unlikeable. That was the exact intention of the documentary, of course, and it conformed to most true-crime media by treating the murderer with extreme prejudice and regarding the defence with extreme hostility. But even though the cross-examination scene was presented to make Mansfield look bad, it was a reminder that he really did have a habit of going too far, that he never left well enough alone, that he did as he pleased. There was no senior counsel to offer advice or temper his approach. He was the boss. He took control of a case and held on to it. When court was in recess, he relaxed, expressed an antic wit, was even quite sensitive and kind of adorable; certainly he was always generous in handing around his big paper bag full of almonds each day; but no one could ever tell him what to do.

His right-hand man at the Polkinghorne trial, Harrison Smith, was no slouch. He disappeared for a day to defend Auckland provocateur Pebbles Hooper at the District Court and kept her out of jail. But it felt wildly improbable he would ever challenge his boss. Smith was only allowed to lead evidence in chief from one witness at the Polkinghorne trial and from my perspective he made a bit of a hash of it; his hands shook, and when the judge gently admonished him for his questioning, he blushed bright red. I felt it wasn't the witness who made him so anxious. It was performing in court next to Ron Mansfield.

Another lawyer at the Polkinghorne trial featured in *The Lie*: Brian Dickey. His prosecution of Jesse Kempson was maybe his finest hour, definitely a career highlight in his years as Crown solicitor. The film showed him in his pomp, a serious, grave figure of authority, filled with a kind of puritanical rage against Kempson, and a resolve to prove his guilt. I joined a queue to shake his hand after the verdict. He accepted each congratulation without joy. It had been his solemn duty. He was all clean, sharp lines throughout the Kempson trial, clearly drawn. I missed that version of Brian Dickey at the Polkinghorne trial. It was as though he never quite found the right shape. I felt he was blurry, not entirely there. Something was missing; hard to think of such a languid fellow suffering from stress, but maybe some kind of anxiety eroded his natural confidence. It was always going to be a hard case to get over the line. He was making a comeback after standing down as Crown solicitor, and he did not seem entirely, as my lawyer friend described Mansfield, trial fit. But one day, during a cross-examination of an expert witness Mansfield had called to tell the court about a mysterious strip of blood, the court got to see Dickey roused to his full powers.

Mysterious, as in complete bullshit, Dickey argued, finally given licence to do what he used to do so well as a Crown solicitor: yell his head off, really go at someone, frighten and bully and upset. The subject was the strange case of a Louisiana crime scene examination expert flying to Auckland two years after Pauline's death and discovering something that had eluded police and ESR — a bloodstain at the bottom of the stairs in Polkinghorne's home. It was Polkinghorne's blood. It would explain the cut — 'the abrasion', the 'scrape' — on his forehead on the morning of

Pauline's death. He had hit his head on the stairs without realising it in a white-out of panic when untying the rope from his wife. Timothy Scanlan, who appeared on video link, said the stain tested positive for Polkinghorne's DNA.

But staining in that area had in fact already been tested by ESR. They did not detect any blood. Police photographed the stain. Scanlan photographed it, too. The images were compared in court. Dickey said the comparison was odious on account of the fact they did not look the same. 'One's got a single line and one's got a parallel line,' he said. 'These are two different lines, aren't they?'

Scanlan said it was the same length and position as in the original photo.

Dickey asked, 'Are we dealing with obvious scene contamination?'

'I think it's a possible explanation,' Scanlan replied, 'but not the only explanation.' They could have been smudged. Two years is a long time in the history of a house. Things happen.

'They are different lines, aren't they?'

'They are different in appearance, yes,' said Scanlan.

I ran into the prosecution team a few days later at lunch at Old Government House. It always surprised me they would eat there. I liked the lentil soup, but everything else on offer was mainly fairly dismal cabinet food. Dickey is a member of the nearby Northern Club; I would have expected they'd choose from the very fine menu. Anyway, they sat there with their pies and rolls and laughed at the strip of blood on Polkinghorne's stairs, at what they saw as his obvious attempt at planting it to explain the cut on his forehead. They were in a good mood. The trial was going well at that point. But it had gone longer than planned, and Dickey had to leave — he'd booked a trip on a cruise ship sailing around the Baltic Sea. I was in court on his final afternoon and joined the queue to shake his hand and wish him a bon voyage. It was sad to see him go. He had been looking forward to giving the closing address. He was confident, though, that the Crown had done enough, and would get the verdict.

But that was before Dr Stephen Cordner, the murder-naysaying Dr Death, and before another, last-minute defence witness — another pathologist, who said much the same things as Cordner, except even more charmingly, even more winningly.

---

Two forensic pathologists walk into a bar. One is from Christchurch, and has a long, gaunt face, given warmth by a moustache. Another is English, living in Ottawa, with a white fringe raked forward above his pink happy face. They meet at a medical conference in America. They order drinks. If the bar was dead, they'd feel at home; together, they have conducted at least 2000 autopsies. They may or may not make small talk but sooner or later they get around to the thing that consumes their professional lives, the big sleep. Martin Sage, the New Zealander, says to his colleague, Christopher Milroy, 'Have you ever seen a death by compression of the neck with no internal or external injury? Because I've just got one, now.'

The case was the death of Pauline. Their bar-room conversation was relayed at the trial when Milroy was called to give evidence on Day 28 of the seventh week — winter had made way for the darling buds of spring, with wisteria in the High Court courtyard in full feminine flower and the plane trees on Princes Street in light, lovely leaf. Polkinghorne observed the same old crazy season on his feet. He wore pink polka-dot socks that day.

Milroy appeared by video link. His white lab coat hung over the door. Books and papers were scattered in brainy piles in his office. His phone rang; he laughed, and said, 'I'm on call and I'm being paged but I'm going to ignore it. It's never that urgent in forensic pathology.' Death is patient. Then he got down to business and said, 'I would have given cause of death as hanging.' And: 'The most likely cause of death was hanging by partial suspension.' Also: 'I'm aware of ideas about some other form of neck compression, with a cover-up by suspending the victim after death, but I don't have any concerns about having an opinion of death by hanging.'

Milroy came late to the defence case. He provided his report nearly four weeks into the trial. He was approached to bolster the defence case after Cordner's findings were challenged by Martin Sage, the moustachioed pathologist who was Milroy's drinking buddy in an American bar. Over their drinks they talked about how the ligature marks around Pauline's neck had disappeared. Milroy said in court, 'The point is that it's not an injury. It is simply an impression. We'd expect it to disappear.'

The more profound issue, he said, was the lack of internal or external injuries to Hanna's neck. It was this absence which occasioned Sage's conversation starter with Milroy over a drink. The two forensic pathologists agreed that the lack of neck injuries in a homicide was an extremely rare event. Sage could only think of one case in his entire career. Milroy could only think of one, too. The victim was a fourteen-year-old girl put in a choke hold. But in all other cases — in his own experience, and in the literature — every single strangling death caused internal or external neck injuries. There were none on the surface of Hanna's neck. Mansfield asked Milroy, 'Did Kilak Kesha dissect her neck to look for internal injuries?'

He replied, 'Correct.'

'And he found none?'

'Correct.'

Milroy's white hair fell forward in two strips, like an 11 on his head. He was almost cherubic. He said, 'If I have concerns about a suicide by hanging, I will do an internal exam, and if I don't find anything, an absence of injuries, that makes me more confident of a suicidal hanging.' His smile indicated he was very confident indeed. He spoke fluently, and in perfect sentences. Cross-examined by Alysha McClintock, though, he ummed and ahhed, and smiled considerably less.

McClintock had argued that Polkinghorne may have attacked Pauline while she was heavily sedated on alcohol and an anti-depressant drug. She put the combination to Milroy: 'A double whammy, if you like.'

He did not like. He replied, 'Well, one interacts with the other.'

She questioned him on how much alcohol Pauline had in her blood. Milroy said tests determined it was at a low level at the time of death. 'We can be confident of that,' he said.

She asked, 'But not when she went to bed?'

He could not be confident. 'No,' he said.

She returned to her theory that Hanna was attacked and unable to struggle. Milroy agreed that it's possible for a victim to lose consciousness after only ten to fifteen seconds if thorough and consistent pressure is placed on the neck. She asked if it took another three or four minutes to cause death. He said, 'I think that's a bit long. I think it's shorter. A minute or two.'

A life extinguished, quickly and brutally. Milroy was asked by both McClintock and Mansfield if he had ever known of a case where a homicidal strangling was performed by a surgeon. He did not. He was also asked if a surgeon would have the requisite forensic experience to know how to strangle someone without leaving internal or external injuries. He laughed at that one. Surgeons were clueless, he implied. 'I would not expect a non-forensic practitioner,' he said, 'to have any skills in that area.'

Just as Cordner dismissed the Crown suspicion of the fast-disappearing ligature mark as a shibboleth, so too had Milroy done away with the theory that Polkinghorne, as a qualified surgeon, a medic of long standing, would know how to throttle Pauline to death in a manner that would mask signs of his fatal attack. Both notions, they said, were fantasies.

It ended there. The long-winded Mansfield managed to keep going; the last little drops of evidence were squeezed out a week later, at 12.26 p.m. on a Friday, Day 31 of the trial at the High Court of Auckland, that bottomless well of pain. 'As it pleases the court,' said Mansfield, even as his final witness was still plodding his way out of courtroom 11, 'that is the defence for Dr Polkinghorne.' It pleased the court very much. Everyone could leave early and enjoy a long weekend. But the *wahala* went with us, followed us home. Before the defence began, Justice Lang turned to the jury, and said, 'We are getting to the sharp end of the trial. There's a long way to go so keep an open mind. Don't come to any conclusions at this stage; it's far too early for that.' Now that the defence had finished, he said much the same thing again. 'You have heard a vast morass of evidence. But please don't come to any conclusions. Mull over by all means what you've heard. We have reached the most critical point of the trial.' The 'sharp end', the 'most critical point'; he was not so much ratcheting up the tension but recognising it as a fact, calling for grace under pressure.

I took the opportunity to leg it out of court to Britomart and caught the eastern line train heading south to Manukau. My friend Luke Radich, a very fine prosecution lawyer, was being made a judge. I wrote a story about the final week of the trial on my phone and was only dimly aware of the train calling in at stations at Glen Innes, Panmure, Papatoetoe; I kept writing when I took my seat at the Manukau District Court and waited for the swearing-in ceremony. I got there early. The room filled until it was standing-room only, and there were a lot of people standing. There was a lot of singing, too; it was a Pasifika event, warm-hearted and beautiful, and the speeches were funny, poignant and respectful. The whole thing was a wonderful reminder of the esteem in which criminal justice is held, and how important it is in a community, a society, a nation. They are matters of life and death, of truth and resolution. The Polkinghorne trial was such a long, crazy spectacle — the lurid socks, the $296,646.23 hooker bill, the 'mind-boggling' allegation of hoaxing a suicide, the whole eight weeks of it — but it was also the usual solemn awfulness of a murder trial, a man accused of the usual, solemn, awful violence against women. He was being tried in a court of law. He was being held to account in the most carefully regulated office in civilisation. It all came down to the evidential perception of

Dr Philip Polkinghorne. *He* was the 'sharp end', *he* was 'the most critical point'; everything about the trial centred on the little bald ophthalmologist who only ever wanted the world to regard him as good old Polky.

CHAPTER 9

# Philip

We have to talk about Polky. And we did, incessantly, during the eight weeks in courtroom 11, sometimes kindly, but mainly with dislike, with harsh and outright contempt for his perceived failings as a human being. There was the Crown projection of Polkinghorne as a killer and a liar and a drug pig — the malignant sex dwarf, diabolical and appalling. There was the defence assurance that Polkinghorne was a grieving widower, an upright member of the community, who was, at worst, 'a silly old fool', in Ron Mansfield's facile observation. And there was the actual Polkinghorne who sat in court, his resting face set in the unfortunate expression of a dimwit, with his lower lip sticking out above a quite absent chin, and who was chatty and likeable when the jury left the room — one of the security guards liked him so much that the two of them sat together laughing and touching each other on the arm during the first week of the trial. He was replaced by other guards but reappeared towards the end of the ordeal and they greeted each other like old friends, Polkinghorne asking after his health, chiding him for not seeing a doctor, putting his hand on the man's shoulder. Most of the ladies and gentlemen of the press ignored him. I treated him like an office colleague, which was a fair summary of our relationship — we saw each other from Monday to Friday in the same dark room parched by air conditioning, were ruled by the same timetable of lunch and tea breaks. 'Morning, Phil.' But it went further than that. I liked him. We exchanged gifts. I brought in a tray of freshly baked banana muffins in the last week of the trial and made sure to include Polkinghorne when I shared them around. I also gave him a French Earl Grey teabag. 'My favourite!' he exclaimed. 'I know,' I said. 'It came up in your police interview.' I had found one when tidying up the cupboards one weekend and thought of him. He was forever in my thoughts. I doubt it was reciprocal. On the morning that Mansfield called forensic pathologist Professor Stephen Cordner to tell the court that he would have ruled Pauline's death as a hanging, Polkinghorne presented me with a pencil. 'Little message for you,' he said, and winked. The pencil had a slogan printed on its side. It read WRITE THAT SHIT DOWN.

Every journalist carries around a deep paranoid fear that another journalist will beat them to a story, gain better access, find something they hadn't even thought to pursue. That paranoia was a clear and present danger all throughout the Polkinghorne trial. I thought it every morning when I took my designated seat in court next to TVNZ reporter Kim Baker Wilson; I scowled at his long, graceful fingers, wondered what unknown truths they were typing. To my left sat *Herald* detective Carolyne Meng-Yee, who knew all but kept it to herself. Further to my right, Catrin Owen from *Stuff* was forever meeting lawyers and police in discreet corners of the High Court. The unexpected arrival of *Listener* editor Kirsty Cameron only deepened my anxieties. She had a watchful, intelligent demeanour and I saw her sometimes having intense conversations with witnesses at QC's café in the courtyard. She was only going to write one story about the trial, she said, and it wouldn't appear until after the verdict. I worried about her better access, her discoveries. The story, when it appeared, was an elegant summary of the trial, written with intelligence and feeling; subtly, cleverly, she withheld something until the last third of her long feature article. We had chatted and texted quite a lot during the trial. Her story was the first time I learned that she knew Polkinghorne personally.

Well, as a kid, and even then, only barely, but her account provided an interesting insight into Polkinghorne's formative years. 'I spent many school holidays popping in to the Polks,' she wrote; she would stay with her grandparents in Tauranga, neighbours and good friends with a Catholic couple, accountant John Polkinghorne and his wife Mary, who raised three children. 'Philip was the middle child, the adored only son whom childhood friends recall as being wilful, prone to literally stamping his foot if he didn't get his way. "I think they were all a bit scared of him," recalls one. "He was spoilt from the day he was born."' Hm. She also wrote, 'One memory remains seared in my mother's mind.' The drama amounted to the young Polkinghorne's idea of a present to give Kirsty when she was born: 'He leaned over my pram and presented his gift — an introduction to his pet rat.' Hm, but not really. This isn't the revealing sinister childhood of a Jeffrey Dahmer, dissecting roadkill as an insane pastime; Polkinghorne belonged to an ordinary New Zealand family and enjoyed an ordinary New Zealand childhood. He was a student at Tauranga Boys' College who thought about becoming a marine biologist but decided on medicine at Otago University, married and had three children, worked long hours as an eye surgeon and struck a goldmine as the co-founder of private ophthalmology practice Auckland Eye.

He belonged to history only as a rank-and-file descendant of colonialism. His name derived from an estate in the parish of Gwinear, Cornwall, recorded as Polkenhoern in 1316 ('pol' was Cornish dialect for pool or pond). Papers Past records the various perambulations of early Polkinghorne arrivals in New Zealand: the first wave heading to Thames following the gold rush of 1872, begetting an Alfred Polkinghorne who was the first of his name to appear in the courts. He pressed assault charges against a Robert Adams in Waihi in 1912. Adams punched Polkinghorne in the mouth, damaging his false teeth. His assailant had the courage to join the famous Waihi strike of 1912. He came across Polkinghorne in an Auckland bar on Christmas Eve. Polkinghorne made 'sarcastic remarks about Adams living on charity, referring to his drawing strike pay'. Adams called him a scab and smashed his face in.

There is a more virtuous Papers Past entry in 1967. A Constable Polkinghorne bravely rescued two kids who fell down a bluff while rabbit hunting in Mangaweka and crossed a treacherous river to find the bodies of two other children, aged six and eight, who fell to their deaths. There is also a glowing obituary for an A.P. Polkinghorne in 1926: 'His name will go down in the history of the Post and Telegraph Department as the engineer who laid in New Zealand the successful foundation of the telegram.' The only other reference is to an unsavoury, but apparently not uncommon 1940s pastime in Whangārei. Gordon Polkinghorne appeared in court in Whangārei in 1942 charged with committing a grossly indecent act one night in a phone box. The judge recorded his disgust: 'The Bench takes a serious view of this type of offence which has become frequent in Whangārei.' Police withdrew the charge — they had shone a torch through the phone booth, and what they saw was in doubt — but he was found guilty of an alternate charge of 'committing a nuisance'. Eighty years later, Philip Polkinghorne would stay the night in Whangārei and search his phone for the names and details of local escorts.

It might seem gratuitous to jot down that latter fact, with its message that everything about Polkinghorne always comes down to sex. Sex became a governing principle of his life but it was hardly the *only* thing going on in his life. He was also accused of another monomania in his methamphetamine use, that he was always on it, a functioning but pathetic junkie. But even given the prospect of duomania — two addictions, two derangements, the twin jet engines of sex and drugs blowing his mind with touch, pleasure, exhilaration, power, altered states — no one is ever one thing or even two things. Everyone has sides. Polkinghorne emerged throughout the trial as someone with a lot of good qualities. One of the truest portraits drawn of him was when he was at ease, on holiday in his summer house in Rings Beach, Coromandel.

The feel of lovely endless Kiwi summers wafted into courtroom 11 whenever Rings Beach was mentioned. We heard how Polkinghorne was very fondly regarded by other bach owners — this was the first time his superb nickname, Polky, was aired in court. He loved it there; the names of the days blurring and meaningless; everything ordered by tides, not time; taking over a bottle to call in on neighbours who would in turn call in on Polky and Pauline with a bottle. Christmas, New Year, Easter. He got up at dawn, long before Pauline woke up, to dive or fish. He packed supplies for the three-hour drive from Auckland, shopping for quality wines, meats, cheeses and other treats at Farro, only needing to stock up on basics at the local store. Everyone in New Zealand knows those holidays, that small-town bliss by sea and sand. Auckland poet Kendrick Smithyman chose small words to get the essence of it in his poem set in Coromandel, 'Colville 1964':

> The sort of place where you stop
> long enough to fill the tank, buy plums
> perhaps, and an icecream thing on a stick
> while somebody local comes
> in, leans on the counter, takes a good look
> but does not like what he sees of you

It was Stephen MacIntyre, the Rings Beach neighbour who became concerned at Polkinghorne's 'erratic' and 'irrational' behaviour and who told the court he was worried his friend was on drugs, who immortalised the name he was known as at Coromandel. Everyone at Rings Beach, he said, called him Polky. 'He was a very intelligent, funny, witty, generous man. We had a lot of laughs together.' Another friendly neighbour from the same idyllic white-sand bay, Dominic Foote, was called by the defence. He had zero concerns about Polkinghorne's behaviour. He saw no reason to think his mate was off his head. Foote was Kiwi joker incarnate, all yeah-gidday and aw-yeah demotic, clinging easily to 1950s values of family, fishing and beer. 'Polky, some call him,' he said, with a smile. 'He was great. Kind, generous. Fantastic to my kids. Yeah. Great neighbour.' He said his family bought a bach two doors down from Polky's summer house in the early 1980s. His parents were friends with Polky and Pauline; he grew up diving and fishing with the couple, and still fishes with Polky to this day, he said. Had he ever seen him act erratically? 'No. He's about as consistent as you get.' Had he ever seen him act in a demeaning and controlling way towards Pauline? 'No. I don't think I've ever seen him raise his voice.' Had he ever seen him drunk, or did he ever worry that he was on drugs? 'No. I don't think I ever saw Philip drunk, but he did enjoy taking a comically large glass of wine around.' We all want people to speak well of us; Foote spoke so well of Polky that it was like love. He said Polky was always in bed at 9.30 p.m.; Brian Dickey seized on this in his cross-examination, and asked, 'How could you know that?' It did seem like intimate knowledge but Foote merely replied, 'Aw, he was like that for two decades. Even on New Year's Eve.' Early to bed, early to rise, a smile on his face every minute he was awake. Yes, he said when Mansfield asked if Polky was funny, he was very funny. 'He's pretty dry. For instance, he kind of had a habit of accidentally sinking his boats, so he started naming them names like the *Bismarck* and the *Lermontov*.' There was a fair bit of laughter in the court and the person who found it funniest was Polky, his shoulders heaving with the hilariousness of his wit back in the day when he was free to dive, to fish, to sink boats in the faraway, long-ago summers at Coromandel. A reprise, from Kendrick Smithyman's evocation:

> A school, a War Memorial
> Hall, the store, neighbourhood of salt
> and hills. The road goes through to somewhere
> else . . .

*Herald* editors added a late update to my online report of the day that Foote appeared as a witness. A line in bold ran along the top. It read, 'This column incorrectly named a witness who was a neighbour of Polkinghorne in the Coromandel as "Simon Foote". The witness's name is "Dominic Simon Foote".' This was a careless mistake, and I had been alerted to it by Simon Foote KC, who emailed:

> Steve. I refer to your article in the *NZ Herald* today about the Polkinghorne murder trial. In the article you report evidence from a defence witness named "Simon Foote", a neighbour of the accused at their Coromandel beach houses. I share that name and by chance have a house on the Coromandel, but I am not the witness.
>
> Mr Mansfield KC tells me the witness's name is in fact "Dominic Foote". I have had numerous inquiries about my

> involvement with Dr Polkinghorne today. I have some profile in the legal community and in particular practice in the criminal courts on occasion as a Crown prosecutor. Whether Dr Polkinghorne is guilty of murder or not, he has admitted drug crimes involving meth and on any reasonable view leads a highly unusual life. It is important to me that people who search for me find correct information. I do not know the accused as "Polky" or at all. He is not a friend or neighbour of mine.
>
> Your article is incorrect as to the name of the witness and has led to confusion and speculation about me. I would be grateful if you would print a correction in bold at the start of your next article as a correction specifying that the Crown witness who is a neighbour of the accused on the Coromandel is not "Simon Foote" but "Dominic Foote". Please provide me with your text for approval as soon as practicable.

Let this book, too, state that Polkinghorne's Coromandel neighbour is not 'Simon Foote' but 'Dominic Foote'; it is important that 'Simon Foote' ought not be associated in any shape or form with 'Polky'.

---

Foote — Simon, not Dominic — was hardly alone in his ambition to distance himself from Polkinghorne. Others likewise regarded him as a plague and were wary of the risk of infection. During the trial, I heard from a classmate of Polkinghorne's at Otago University med school. There was a reunion coming up in Wellington. 'Some have asked he not attend, and he is keen to come (presuming he will be a free man).' As soon as the verdict came in, members of the exclusive Northern Club — up the road from the High Court, its lovely ivy clinging to the stone walls — declared they wanted Polkinghorne thrown out. Lady Deborah Chambers KC told the inevitable Carolyne Meng-Yee at the *Herald* that his continued membership would lower its reputation. 'The evidence at the trial indicated he is not a suitable person to be a member . . . I'm sure people would stand up and walk out if he comes in. I don't want to have dinner with someone like him.' Feelings were similar at a curious little chartered club in the suburb of Glendowie. The Churchill Club has views overlooking the Tāmaki Estuary towards Musick Point. It has quiz nights and fishing contests, and the most controversial issue at its most recent AGM was to note, 'The bar chiller is 35 years old and needs replacing.' In one of my *Herald* stories during the trial, I quoted from an email Polkinghorne had sent to Pauline, in early 2020: 'Off to Churchill Club in Glendowie.' After the verdict, the club contacted the newspaper to complain. Polkinghorne, it stated, was not a member. The modern history of newspapers is to recognise there are many hills not worth dying on and it discreetly removed the reference online. It pleased the Churchill Club. Distance, achieved; the plague of association, avoided.

One of the first things we learn in adversity is who our friends aren't. The ones who run for cover, who lack that useful thing known as a spine. Ron Mansfield told the jury that Polkinghorne pretty much didn't have a friend in the world after police began investigating Pauline's death. The police officer in charge of ogling at sex videos, sexts and whatever else on Polkinghorne's phone, Detective Andrew Frame, confirmed in cross-examination that the only person outside of Polkinghorne's family who regularly messaged him was Madison Ashton. Everyone else had deserted him, or so it seemed. Mansfield was able to call on three people — loyal, faithful — to the witness box and say nice things about his client. 'His patients loved him,' said Sharon Jenkins, a receptionist at Auckland Eye. 'He always treated his patients really well. Some patients didn't always have the money to pay for their consults and he'd pay for them.' Leonie Darlington was a colleague for eighteen years: 'He was very good to work with, he was a perfectionist . . . Quite a dry sense of humour, always ready for a laugh . . . He was very considerate . . . Some patients couldn't afford the procedure . . . He'd sometimes forgo his surgeon's fee as the procedure needed to be done.' Jillian Blakely was a colleague for 27 years: 'He always had the patients' best interests at heart . . . I really enjoyed working with him . . . Cheeky . . . Dedicated . . . Always very supportive.' She ended with the compliment all Kiwi men crave above all else: 'A good guy.'

Workmates who had known him for eighteen years, for 27 years — these are the people who know us best, who see us day in, day out in the controlled experiment of capitalism known as the office. So much of the Polkinghorne story — his role as a doctor at Auckland Eye, his wife's job at Counties Manukau DHB — was about work. The word itself appears here for the ninety-fifth time. Mr and Mrs Polky were executive class, which is to say they worked their guts out to earn the comforts and securities of the good life. Pauline emailing all night for work; Pauline never looking less than immaculate at work; Pauline dealing with Covid vaccine roll-outs at work; Pauline having regular catch-ups with the so-called 'Middlemore Housewives', her women friends from work. Polkinghorne snoring off at a boring Zoom meeting at work; Polkinghorne agitated and anxious over his payout from all his years of service at work; Polkinghorne being generous to patients at work; Polkinghorne being funny and dedicated and supportive to others at work. You can fool your friends, but you can't fool the people you work with, who you swim with in the transparent fishtank of nine to five. Easy to imagine the bow-tied Polkinghorne walking into the office and lighting up that awful place, beset with defections and massive payouts in 2019. 'Morning, Phil!'

You could see him reflected, too, in the eyes of someone not quite a friend or a work colleague, but who played an indispensable, even intimate role in the lives of his clients: Tony Glucina, Polkinghorne's investment advisor. He was called as a defence witness to talk money. Money was his area of expertise. Money followed him into the witness box and buttoned his beautiful black suit from Crane Brothers. Money was the only thing he talked about for quite a long time; he was asked few questions, but answered at length, in a loud and confident voice, explaining exactly what it is he did for a living as a private wealth advisor at JBWere and in his former position at Goldman Sachs, where he focused on equity and debt issuance, mergers and acquisitions, corporate advisory, public market takeovers, US private placements and other capital market transactions. There was something godlike about him. Here was someone who had the divine power to make you rich. The only catch is that you had to be rich in the first place. He made Polkinghorne richer. He talked about 'a good allocation to global investments' and 'providing capital growth to retirement'. He said he invested Polkinghorne's money into Apple, Amazon and other large multinationals. Polkinghorne's portfolio had done well, reaching $2.2 million. And yet the strongest message of Glucina's evidence had nothing to do with money. In fact, it was wordless. It happened twice. He raised his eyebrows at Polkinghorne in the Kiwi gesture of mateship when he took his seat in the witness box and smiled at him with a tilt of his head on the way out. Everyone saw it. They were deep, simple displays of support and affection. He was recognising a different kind of Polkinghorne, completely separate to the Crown's caricature of a slobbering Mr Hyde; he was tilting his head at Doc Polky, good guy.

In any case he *had* put it into words, describing a dinner he had with Polky and Pauline at their Rings Beach house in January 2021, just two months before Pauline died. Asked how the two of them behaved, he replied, 'Like a normal couple. Philip is quite a flamboyant, interesting person to talk to, always cracked a few jokes.' Polky took pride in showing Glucina around the house. He said he had been diving that day. He said they didn't have TV, and they enjoyed reading together late into the night . . . Just a nice old guy at ease on a summer's day in January. The only ominous note was Pauline's behaviour. She seemed stressed about work, Glucina said, and didn't eat a bite of their three-course meal, didn't so much as touch it. It was his wife who noticed. 'She's a well-known naturopath and nutritionist,' he told the court, meaning Buffy Ellen Gill, author of the 2022 cookbook *Be Good: Plant-Based Recipes for Everybody* and who has 42,400 followers on Insta. There were times when the Polkinghorne trial was like a parable of the Auckland way of life.

I ran after Glucina when he left court. I was struck by his overt show of support for Polkinghorne, his loyalty. The first thing he said was, 'Are you George Block?' When I caught up with him in the outdoor courtyard, he was reading about himself on George's live blog in the *Herald* and marvelling at the speed of reporting what he had only just finished saying in courtroom 11. He was disappointed I was someone he had never heard of but tolerated one question. I asked, 'What do you make of Polky?' He shook his head, and said, 'I didn't know about all this other stuff. The sex workers. Meth. But, you know, so what? I mean — where's the evidence? There's no evidence.' There was so much else I wanted to ask him, for instance about that dinner in Rings Beach, but I was so dazzled by his height and his suit that I gabbled, 'I love your suit. Where'd you buy it?' He said, 'Crane Brothers.' And with that he gapped it, travelling even faster than George's live blog, covering all of Parliament Street in one bound of his very long legs.

The Polkinghornes were like a model of Auckland wealth, indexed by the kinds of people they employed: witnesses included their hairdressers, their accountant, Pauline's doctor, Polkinghorne's sex staff, their investment advisor, their personal trainer. Barry Payne trained them both. He appeared as a prosecution witness but really he gave Polkinghorne a very favourable review. 'Philip was a knowledgeable, interesting man.' And then he quoted one particular message that felt like a key to understanding Polkinghorne, to getting a sense of his essential self, his boundless energies, the joy he took in his physical existence. It was from the last time he saw them for a workout, on the Saturday morning of that fatal Easter 2021. Polkinghorne texted, 'Hi Barry I am on fire. Intend to break every record. I will be there at 9.'

To the Crown, this was evidence of the bang and boost of methamphetamine. But it sounds exactly like Polkinghorne in his natural state — the braggart, motivated and up for it, wanting to revel in the performance and endurance of his body. He was the sort of guy who made himself known in every room, a fit, lively presence, always on the move. Madison Ashton posted photos of Polkinghorne in their Sydney love nest. He was shirtless or draped in loose-fitting gowns. The biceps were well developed, he had wide shoulders, his tum looked taut. He had trained with Payne twice a week for fifteen years at CityFitness in Newmarket. Payne also trained Pauline, for eight years. The couple often talked about him in their messages to each other — 'Off to see Bazz', 'Great session with Bazza', etc. The bond with personal trainers is intimate. They know our bodies better than our doctors do. There's an excitement, a shared mission. Payne and Polkinghorne had a friendly, jokey competition about how many push-ups they could do — Polkinghorne performed a very creditable 30. Strength and fitness are admirable goals, and they demand honesty. To Payne, Polkinghorne showed no signs of drug abuse; his client shed weight, about 8 kilograms in 2017 or 2018 he reckoned, and kept it off for the remaining years, and he put it down entirely to his diet.

'He was training quite well but as I say you had to diet to get it off rather than train it off.'

Mansfield, in cross-examination: 'You'd be pretty chuffed with that outcome?'

'Absolutely.'

As for Pauline, she trained well, too, he said, but constantly late. 'I've never had anyone who's like that.' Late to arrive, and sometimes early to leave, to work 'on the Covid thing'. Asked if she appeared to be suffering the strains of work, he said, 'She seemed

... haggard is not the word ... but run down, I would say. Pauline could be a little bit ... moody's the word. She could be uptight.'

Not so Polkinghorne. He was steady, committed. He felt the burn for fifteen long years and would often arrive early for their hour-long session, using the time by warming up on the treadmill. He'd then push tin. Payne inculcated Polkinghorne with the motto 'Use it or lose it'. He drummed it in to all his clients, mostly older guys in their fifties to seventies. 'For a man of his age he trained very, very well,' said Payne, a long-limbed man with a slightly verbose manner. Language wasn't something he controlled very well. Words got away with him and he chased them all around the courtroom in his brief but memorable appearance. Memorable, for his obvious good opinion of Polkinghorne despite appearing as a prosecution witness; memorable, for the text that he quoted with its passion and ambition: 'I am on fire. Intend to break every record.'

The couple had booked an appointment on Easter Monday. Pauline was due to arrive at 9 a.m., followed by Polkinghorne. Payne was sitting around his home in gym gear about to head to CityFitness when Polkinghorne phoned him at 8:36 a.m. That was unusual; he only ever texted him. The first thing he said was, 'She's dead, she's dead.' Polkinghorne was wailing, sobbing. Payne asked if he was joking. Polkinghorne said he wasn't joking. He said, 'She is gone Barry, she's gone.'

Payne said, incredibly, 'Did she sleep in?'

Polkinghorne replied, 'No, Barry, she's dead. She's taken her own life.'

They ended the call. Payne told his partner what had happened. She asked if he had expressed his deepest sympathies to Polkinghorne. Payne seemed slow on the uptake that morning and admitted he had not, so he called him back. They agreed to meet up soon. 'See you later in the week, we'll have a coffee, go over it,' Polkinghorne said, as though organising a catch-up.

Payne reached out to him two days later. Polkinghorne texted, 'At the moment I can't do anything but weep. I'm an absolute mess.' But his absolutism was not, you know, absolute. There was always that one other thing to consider, that one distracting need that burnt the soles of his feet and got him moving, awake, up for it, that did not contradict grief or negate it or expose it as shocking hypocrisy or an outright lie but worked with it, gave it another, inevitable layer, in his wildly expressive character — 'Hi, I know it's late,' he texted a week after Pauline died, on 12 April, 11.56 p.m., to Rachel, the sex worker across the harbour bridge in Northcote, where neighbours got used to seeing him pull up on Friday afternoons in his big white Merc with the licence plate RETINA, 'but I was thinking of visiting later?'

So, yes, always back to sex with Polkinghorne, sex always. There it was, only hours after Pauline died, the subject coming up in the College Hill police station that afternoon when he was asked about the last time he had sex with his wife, and he said they had sex every day. So much sex; he couldn't be expected to remember. 'I think it was Sunday morning,' he mused, sitting with his legs wide apart. Story by Carolyne Meng-Yee in the *Herald*, a week after the verdict:

> An international porn star and escort claims Philip Polkinghorne contacted her two days after his wife Pauline Hanna died. US-based Kiwi Aubrey Black claims the now-retired Auckland eye surgeon offered her Hanna's designer

> shoes, a handbag and the use of her Mercedes after one of their $3000 sessions . . . Polkinghorne booked another escort in July 2021 and took her skydiving in Queenstown. During the August 2021 Covid lockdown the woman had stayed with him at his Rings Beach holiday house for a month. The sex worker says he treated her as his "lockdown wife" and was sexually demanding.

But all this is to give way to yet another recitation of his sex life. We get the picture. He had sex a lot. He was a prisoner of sex. (I tried this on in one of my *Herald* despatches but was met with a cautious rejoinder from a sub: 'On legal advice we've been asked to rephrase "prisoner of sex" as it seems to prejudge the outcome of the trial.') Inevitably it says something about his need to control — sex as power — but it goes beyond that, speaks to a sense of freedom. Weird to haul in Queen Victoria, of all people, to shed light on Polkinghorne, but Lytton Strachey's observation of the monarch as a child is useful: 'By nature impulsive, capricious and vehement, she had always longed for liberty; and she had never possessed it.' It recalls the description of Polkinghorne that childhood friends gave to *Listener* editor Kirsty Cameron as 'wilful, prone to literally stamping his foot if he didn't get his way . . . spoilt from the day he was born'. He got his way with the wonderful availability of sex workers — only a phone call away — and the morally transgressive exhilarations of group sex. They offered freedom from the boring normative social codes of his Remuera cohort. Camille Paglia very often got at some elemental truth of men and women in her various writings on sexual politics and Polkinghorne is illuminated by the torch of one of her epigrams.

'Straight men who visit prostitutes are valiantly striving to keep sex free from emotion, duty, family — in other words, from society, religion, and procreative Mother Nature.' Polkinghorne was raised Catholic. Sex freed him from God as thoroughly as it freed him from the bonds of New Zealand puritanism. But there was another, personal freedom. Sex offered a great escape from something that turned him into a dark and stormy Mr Hyde, even more than methamphetamine or any kind of artificial stimulant. Throughout the trial, he was described as an angry sonofabitch.

---

The famous Longlands tape, the recording of a conversation between Pauline and her family over dinner, immortalised Pauline's highly original term for her husband's anger: she said numerous times on tape that when his mood turned, when he got dark, it put him on a place she identified as 'on the roof'. Strange phrase. It's probably a variation of someone hitting the roof, but maybe aiming higher, breaking through the ceiling and emerging wild and raving on top of the damned gables, a visible and dangerous platform for someone to lose their shit. Polkinghorne on the roof was Polkinghorne beside himself with rage. He would lash out at Pauline with cruel and cutting assessments. He would not climb down off the roof. He would stay up there, unpredictable and savage — like Queen Victoria, 'impulsive, capricious and vehement'.

Again and again, Crown prosecution pointed to his anger as a sure sign he was capable of killing his wife. Something in him snapped, Alysha McClintock told the jury in her opening and closing addresses, on the night of Pauline's death. He lost it. He got angry. He bounded on the roof. The classic precedent was Pheasant Riordan's demonstration of Polkinghorne putting his hands around Pauline's neck and hissing at her that he could do that any time he wished. This was Polkinghorne as that favourite tabloid psychological metaphor, the ticking time bomb, one spark away from the ultimate transgression of taking someone's life.

Pauline, at Longlands:

> He gets very wound up. He's someone who does not handle stress. He's out of control. He's been revolting. He's controlling. He had a go at me in Paris and at the beach. On Sunday, Philip turned on me. He told me all the things I'm not. I cried the whole fucking night. I cried my eyes out . . . He's a very complex character. He's just such a sex fiend. He doesn't know how to control himself.

Her running commentary on Polkinghorne 'on the roof' was entirely separate from witnesses who spoke about his displays of rage in the office, and over dinner one night at the Northern Club. Both of those incidents were expressions of his bitter, crushed feeling that Auckland Eye were screwing him out of hundreds of thousands of dollars in his payout. But they were further instances of a man who kept his emotions close to the surface, who was a creature driven by mood, whim, temper. He was all over the place. Pauline also said at Longlands, 'He does love me and he's lost without me. He becomes so remorseful, and he cries.' He cried four or five times at the trial. He cried when a cop presented an exhibit: the braided leather belt Polkinghorne said was around

Pauline's neck. For the rest of the trial, it lay coiled like a thin dry snake on a table next to a carafe of water. He cried loudest right at the very end of the trial when the jury came back from their deliberations and asked to hear the 111 call for the second time.

'What is your emergency?'
'My wife's dead. She's hung herself.'
'She's hung herself, is that correct?'
'Yes. Yes.'
'Cut her down immediately.'
'Cut her down. Cut her down. Yeah.'
'Can you cut her down?'
'Yep . . .'

They always play 111 calls in court at top volume, the amp turned to *Spinal Tap* 11, a howl of static and breath, of sob and stutter; it makes it all the more harrowing to listen to. Polkinghorne lost it; he did not merely weep in sorrow and grief but howled out loud, really went for it, made a spectacle of himself. The jury were all set to reach their verdict.

He cried, too, in the long police interview at College Hill. That seemed entirely natural and credible. His wife had died that morning. The trouble with the interview is that almost nothing else seemed natural or credible or normal. It was an epic rave, the worst police interview I had ever seen — 'Same,' said one of the prosecutors, who added that there was no way they would instruct Polkinghorne to give evidence if he was their client. He covered so many subjects. There was a plot synopsis of *New Amsterdam*; he and Pauline had watched it on her last night alive. He spoke about Auckland roadworks, chilly bins, vials, vaccinations, cricket, memory, social media ('We're not Facebook people'), tea, toast, chops, wine ('Sometimes, if she's very lucky, I'm standing at the top of the stairs holding a glass of wine for her'), an intruder, wanting to see Pauline's body at the mortuary, the temperature in the room ('I'm shivering') . . . It got so crazy that some members of the jury started laughing. One explanation for it that struck everyone who watched it was that this was what methamphetamine sounded like, that Polkinghorne was off his face. 'I can't say that,' Alysha McLintock said on-camera in the documentary series *Polk*. She was being coy. You could tell it was *exactly* what she meant. And maybe that was the simple truth of it. He was on drugs.

And yet, and yet. Mansfield told the jury that Polkinghorne would not give evidence because he had already said everything about Pauline's death in the police interview, and everything he said had checked out. Mansfield was right. Any expectation that the Crown would find so many inconsistencies that they could drive a truck through it — standard prosecution practice in murder trials — never came to pass. Small example: the ottoman in Pauline's bedroom was tipped on its side. It suggested a struggle, a fight. Polkinghorne said he had stood on it to reach soft toys in a cupboard. It tipped over when he got off it. His shoes matched a print on the ottoman and police photos picked out the soft toys in Pauline's bedroom; she had wanted them for when Polkinghorne's grandchildren would visit. It checked out. Everything checked out. Every single detail, corroborated. None of it exposed as an outright lie or a complete falsehood. It had been a long and intense interview. He hadn't eaten all day — a muffin bought for him by police lay half-eaten on the table. And throughout, for all his ravings, he said nothing the Crown could take apart.

It included his account, given in considerable detail, about the before and after Pauline's death.

Before:

> On Easter Sunday, I made Pauline breakfast and she had that and because it was a fine day, she decided to wash a whole lot of stuff. So the place looks a little bit like a laundry that day. I'm not quite sure what I did in the morning after that, I worked and I know we met for lunch. Pauline wanted to do something. She asked me to take a car home, which I did, then I think I worked in the afternoon and I suspect Pauline did too.

After he found her body and called 111:

> I was trying to put her down flat. I think they told me to do that. As I did so, I dropped the phone. I was sobbing uncontrollably. It was just like having an arm pulled off you. It was horrible. When I got her off the chair, the dressing gown was all over the place. Both arms were in the sleeves but it was open in the front, skew-whiff and half off. It just looked awful.

The detective asked about Pauline's legs. He replied, 'They were going in opposite directions. It looked grotesque really.'

Was Pauline slouched forward in the chair? 'Not quite.' He stood up, got a chair, and sat down on it to act it out. Then he drew a picture.

> I think she was leaning forward like so. I don't think she was sitting all the way back in the chair. Then around her neck was my belt but the belt wasn't that tight, I don't think. I would have thought it had to be tight to do the business, but maybe, I don't know.
>
> I said to someone afterwards, I was surprised the balustrade had taken a dead weight of 70 kg. I don't know whether the knot slipped. I'm just trying to think, why was she sitting there in the chair? Maybe she was standing on a chair and went off and . . . maybe, I don't know. 70 kg on that balustrade, that's a hell of a weight.
>
> The rope was attached to the balustrade above. That was granny knots too, from memory. It looked awful just hanging there. It was offensive to me, the rope.

Detailed, not at all evasive, self-doubting, resolutely and consistently helpful; and within it and around it, mad yap about MacKenzie bread; pillows; phones; staining the deck; the agony of death: 'I knew she was dead straight away. I don't think her face was contorted. I don't think she looked at peace or anything, my God no . . . I thought I saw her breathe, move, sometimes dead people do that.'

It wasn't as though he was unaware of how weird the monologue sounded. He acknowledged that he was 'jumping all over the place', and thought he was probably just as bad when he gave his statement to police at the house that morning: 'The cop who was taking my statement before must have been pulling his hair out.'

I can think of a third such occasion. One day in Week 7 of the trial I loped over to Polkinghorne for a yarn. It was during a long adjournment. He always stood up to talk — he had good manners, never swore, accepted the fact I was there as part of a massive press contingent monetising his trial — and probably shared my motive for a chat, which was to kill time in an agreeable manner. And so he launched into a speech about conservation. 'Every time I see a pine tree, I lose the will to live,' he said. But then he went on, and on, with asides, jokes, fragments, and segued into other subjects, most of it incoherently, just a babble of words. It was baffling, weird, impossible to follow. Kendall Roy, from *Succession*: 'Words are just, what? Nothing. Complicated air flow.'

Anyway, the point I'm trying to make here is that the Polkinghorne monologue was exactly the kind of rubbish he was spouting in the police interview. What seemed so revealing of suspicious behaviour in that little room at the College Hill copshop — Polkinghorne in jeans and a pink shirt, with a white hat beside him on the two-seater couch — now struck me as just the way a slightly crazy, or at least definitely eccentric, guy liked to talk, in random patterns, enthusiastically, fairly disorganised but in no way suggestive that he was some kind of psycho. His preferred method of language was circumlocutory; Polkinghorne, born into a verbose name, was wired to blather.

His nervous energy was a constant. He did not do languid. We venerate our idea of the good Kiwi joker as a man of few words, all of them shrewd, knowing, brief interruptions to the law of good New Zealand silence. Polkinghorne existed on the opposite pole. Throughout the trial I cringed to think of his hopeless chances of a good relationship with the Hanna family while Pauline was alive; they would surely have hated his yap and his bluster, his chit and his chat, felt assailed and repulsed by it, part of their animus towards the man who let loose whatever tirade of abuse at his wife.

But that was Polkinghorne. He talked too much. Everything about him operated in a state of excess. He would not be reined in, he was an artist in constant flow, a beatnik ophthalmologist living out Jack Kerouac's vision, from *On the Road,* of 'the mad ones, the ones who are mad to live, mad to talk, mad to be saved, desirous of everything at the same time, the ones who never yawn or say a commonplace thing, but burn, burn, burn like fabulous yellow roman candles'.

The Merc with the licence plate RETINA, the bow ties he wore to Auckland Eye every day: these trappings were his gaudy suits of armour, his terms of reference. And so, too, he stayed true to his essential self during the eight weeks he was on trial for the murder of his wife with another exhibition of excess: by wearing one pair of crazy socks after another. I made a big deal of it at the trial and for readers it became instantly recognisable, but it was no mere observation of kookiness or quirkiness. They were statement socks, the socks of freedom.

His feet flew flags of the rising sun in painful yellows and reds, crazy socks, loud socks, porno socks. There were socks with grapefruits and socks with moons on them. You don't wear socks like that. You wouldn't dare. But Polkinghorne dared to wear his wild, wild heart on his feet every single day of his trial, in a never-repeated selection: dramatic aqua stripes one day, headache dayglo socks the next. One day, his sister Ruth turned up in court wearing a tribute to her beleaguered brother: a blouse patterned with socks.

The jury couldn't see his socks. They were for his own benefit. I have seen some men accused of murder keep a tight grip on the Bible and others hold fast to the Koran. Polkinghorne's mad socks were his faith, his secret power. They were the devil's socks, Satan slipping on his hose over cloven feet. They were socks that kept him on his toes. The prosecution threw a lurid garment over his shoulders, stitch by stitch knitting ye olde scarlet letter of shame for him to wear; Polkinghorne resisted it, dismissed it as a falsehood, stayed grounded in his socks. He wore his socks on his sleeve. His socks believed in him. His socks put one foot in front of another. His socks talked to him. They spoke in his voice, were chatty and jabbering — he wore circumlocutory socks. They walked him into court on the first day of the trial and they walked him right on out on the final day, the jury sending him home to spend the rest of his days as he wishes. Strange to think of him going about his business both in broad daylight and after dark, the same old crazy Polkinghorne, no doubt bedecked in the same old crazy socks. They will follow him to the grave.

CHAPTER 10

# Lunch with Madison

She went missing, presumed dead silent, when she was expected to give evidence, potentially very, very damaging evidence indeed, in the Auckland High Court murder trial of her former client and, latterly, former de facto romantic partner ('I get to fuck you endlessly'), but she was busily feeding morsels and titbits and assorted revelations to the media while on her travels in Europe, and after it was all over she showed up in Auckland, in person, to keep her appointments with the media to whom she fed more morsels, more titbits, more assorted revelations. I met Madison Ashton for lunch at the Park Hyatt on Auckland's waterfront. I chose the venue. I wanted somewhere posh and discreet.

The place was going off, a riot of blaring trumpets and the rat-tat-tat of drums, hundreds of people, beautiful women in tight little outfits, men in linen suits — I wondered if I had stumbled on a wedding party, but it was much more than that. It was a garish trans-Tasman event that matched my appointment with a visitor from Australia: Melbourne Cup Day.

I arrived fifteen minutes early. So did she. We bumped into each other and there was absolutely no mistaking who it was. Only Madison Ashton looks like Madison Ashton. Even though there was something generic about her cosmetic maximisations — everything large, blown up — she had a natural and touching prettiness to her features. She wore leather pants and a tight blue top. Her nails were painted gold. At 50, she was classy and glamorous, and her manner was friendly, demure, shy.

We sat down and scanned the menu. There wasn't a lot she could eat, as in she couldn't really eat anything; she had recently gone for gastric surgery, and her post-op regime was no solids. We lunched for two hours. She had a ready wit and could be quite epigrammatic; she loved punning 'hierarchy' as 'whorearchy' to discuss her perception of the top echelons of sex workers. She saw herself in that top echelon. She had a belief in herself and her abilities. I felt she was genuine in every single thing she said. She was nobody's fool — but like a lot of people with that determination she was prone to being her own fool, by talking herself up and overestimating her importance. She put up a hell of a front. She needed it. It guarded a person I thought of as terribly vulnerable and terribly lonely. She settled for tom yum soup.

She laughed at the interest the Polkinghorne trial had generated, and said, 'You know, I couldn't believe that it took hold so intensely here. I thought, oh, maybe you guys are just going through a slow news period.'

I said, 'I think this would have been huge any year.'

'But he's not even that rich. He's real estate rich. Like, he bought the house for a mil, and it's appreciated by another four. And he's got, you know, a few investments. But so has the entirety of Parnell and Remuera. And so if you think he's rich, then you must think that half your population is loaded.'

'Well, that's the right arithmetic, because he's how the other half live.'

'Okay so his sex work expenditure was off the chart,' said the main beneficiary of his sex work expenditure. 'He has no intention of changing that, because he's a spendthrift narcissist. I absolutely regard him as a covert narcissist, as a clinically covert narcissist.'

'What are his good qualities?'

She sighed, and her shoulders slumped. 'I liked him a lot in the limited circumstance that we were in. But you think one nice quality means it comes with many nice qualities, and it doesn't. It was obviously in his interest to be nice to me. That's baseline meet and greet.'

'He's funny, though, right?'

'I never found him very funny.'

'But that's his thing, his calling card. "A dry wit", all that. But not funny? Really?'

'No.'

'What did you like about him?'

'That he was a fat chubby nerd and that he had an honest relationship with his wife. I saw a great relationship and I thought to myself, "I would go out of my way for a relationship like that." And I stupidly told him that I thought what they had was great, and that's something that I would like for me if I could find it.'

'What do you mean?'

Our drinks arrived. I ordered a lager, and Madison was given her strawberry margarita.

'Just that he wasn't sexually possessive,' she answered. 'Like most men are like, "You can't have my wife, and I own her and any sharing would be considered unfair or whatever." You know, the checklist. But they didn't live by those rules. And they did it well and they weren't stupid, and they weren't, you know, unemployed or uneducated or anything like that. They were just people who lived a functional life. I thought that was awesome and I was like, "Great. I'd like that." Because I'm never going to give up my occupation for a relationship. I think I should be respected for the occupation that you meet me in, whether you engage in it or not. And he seemed cool with that. Well, how can he not be? He's a consumer of it. You can't have it both ways. I mean, everyone tries it on, but it's unfair to act like, "Oh, I'm a lowly consumer and I have a problem with my partner being a sex worker." Fuck off!'

'But he was never like that.'

'No, he had a fetish for it. He doesn't support me as a sex worker. He supports himself with his never-ending sexual wonderland that exists in his psychopathy. So I basically signed on to a relationship that was a never-ending occupation. I was never a human being. It was just him getting his rocks off in his very fertile mind.'

She was going one way with her memoir of her time with Polkinghorne, but I couldn't help asking if there hadn't been something fun, decent, loving or at least blandly comfortable going on between them. I said, 'Yeah, but did you have nice times outside of the sex?'

Her expression was severe. She said, 'Oh, my God. Everyone asks the same boring fucking question. Okay. Firstly, I was abused before I even knew I was abused. And I was groomed, so any nice times were just a function of abuse.

'I don't want to be asked those questions anymore. You all know the same information. I was lied to and manipulated. So it was all bullshit. So what nice times am I supposed to go on about? What, the nice times that are a ticking time bomb? Those nice times?'

The soup arrived.

---

Very large white prawns floated on the top of her tom yum soup. She used her spoon like an oar to brush them aside and delved only into the hot spicy liquid. 'Lovely,' she said. It restored her good humour, and she said, 'Tell me about those muffins you baked and took to court.'

'Ah yes,' I said. 'The banana muffins.'

'Were they crispy yet soft on the inside? Did you bring butter to the equation?'

'I totally brought the butter.'

'Class act,' she said.

I wasn't about to continue my futile and stupid attempt to quiz her on Polkinghorne's nice qualities. I thought I might gain some insight from her on Pauline. I wasn't sure how many times they had met in Sydney, but I supposed some kind of intimacy or character assessment was achieved in their various threesomes or moresomes, and so I asked, 'What was Pauline like?'

'Pauline was socially very awkward,' she said. 'I think she was on the spectrum or something like that. That's what I was picking up on.'

'Did you get to know her well?'

'No, not at all. How am I supposed to get to know someone at a booking? I'm doing my job. I'm here to, you know, do my service as they've rightfully paid for and expect, you know. But I just found that she just didn't sort of pick up social cues. Very cold, and she wasn't fun to be around.'

Our conversation turned to Polkinghorne's family. 'A classic narcissist's family dynamic,' she pronounced.

'Did you meet Ruth after Pauline had died?'

'No. Ruth came to my house to meet me. We had dinner. She kept up the fantasy and enabled his lie that he was divorced.'

'Did she actually lie about that to your face?'

'Well, she didn't say anything. He's telling her, "This is my partner. We're gonna be together forever." But she knew he was still married and living with Pauline. And then there's Tracey,' she said, meaning Pauline's sister, who gave evidence claiming that Pauline had wanted to kill herself after their father died. 'She's a loser. She's a nothing. I looked at her social media and everything. She's, you know, middle-aged, hefty.'

Everywhere, bitterness. I had seen a preview of it when Madison emailed a screenshot taken on the night of the verdict. It captured a social media post that Ruth had addressed to *Herald* journalist Carolyne Meng-Yee: 'Your are a cunt. Just cos you didn't get an interview.' Madison had stepped in, and replied, 'The best part about all of this, regardless of the verdict, is that you will never ever live this down for the rest of your life . . . You deserve everything that's coming to you.'

The overwhelming tone of it was nastiness. She was very skilled at lashing out, quite fearless; she had no one in her life, nothing to lose. For all her strength, her belief in herself, she was a loner, someone on the margins.

'Basically, I have no friends,' she said. 'I just have really lovely friendly associations. But no close friends anymore. I can't afford it ever. People just cannot behave themselves around me properly in close contact. Regular close contact is just — I just don't want to deal with it anymore.

'But I have a better opportunity to have healthier or pleasant relationships if I'm more aloof and have less contact rather than more contact. Just keep my own space. And that's where the dogs kick in.'

'The chihuahuas.'

'Yeah. And just making sure my finances are completely healthy. Early bedtime, early to rise. Daily exercise.'

'But you must have had mates?'

'All my so-called friends have betrayed me and destroyed me. Narcissists and abusers are incredibly attracted to me. My family of origin has helped me replicate these monsters. I'm too porous and too nice and I wasn't given the awareness or the innate kind of knowledge of how to self-protect because I wasn't protected as a child. My father is not good enough for me as a father. He does not earn or warrant the title father.'

She began to weep.

'Sorry,' I said, and then made matters as bad as they could possibly go when I asked her about her mother.

Madison just stared at me.

'Oh, right. God,' I said, remembering that her mother had died by suicide. 'Sorry.'

---

She kept oaring the succulent prawns aside, and I said, 'I suspect you might not chow down on those prawns.'

She said, 'Well, I'm gonna have a little crack on the crispy edges. But listen, Steve, can I ask you something? Could you just share one tiny, teeny, weeny, itsy-bitsy little chip.'

'Be my guest,' I said and pushed the plate of burger and fries closer towards her. She plucked at one with the tips of her gold nails and slowly sunk it down the hatch like a pelican swallowing a fish. She moaned, 'Oh, God. Oh, my God.'

She closed her eyes. 'You can feel the fat bursting across my taste buds like they're orgasming. It's really good. I love it.'

She swallowed the last of it and moaned harder. 'Oh this chip. Thank you so much. Okay. Oh. My. God.'

We talked a little about the famous photo Norrie Montgomerie took of Polkinghorne in his freaky red pants. She asked him for permission to use it on an anti-Polkinghorne blog she had up and running for a little while; they stayed in touch, and he ended up taking photos of her for her OnlyFans page. 'They were absolutely gorgeous. I've made lots of money off them, so I'm very happy. And so now Norrie has asked me to come with him to a party on Friday night at the Northern Club. I'm like, "Do you reckon?"'

'What do you reckon? You tempted?'

'Yeah, I am, actually,' she said, and laughed.

'You're funny,' I said. 'And you're nice.'

'Really?'

'Yeah.'

'I didn't know that. Okay. Oh, that's good. That's good. Because, you know, I've been through a lot. I had Philips all my life, my entire adult life. Abusers. Gaslighters, underminers. Ne'er do wells.'

I said, 'Mind you, I liked Philip, too, from talking with him in court.'

The ecstasy of the chip had disappeared. 'Any niceness he has to you, just realise you just exist in a narcissistic moment. Don't ever think anything other than you're just being used like toilet paper, a tampon, tyre tread. That's it. You're nothing to him. There is no *him* at all. He gets physical sensations. That's why he likes sex and drugs so much and his job so much because it's all external. There's nothing innate in him. He's dead-eyed. You know, I didn't even want that relationship. I wasn't in a position to take on a full-tilt relationship. But he really, really, really sold it to me. I mean, epic award-winning acting.'

'Did you give a lot of yourself?'

'Of course I did. I was all in. I thought I was going to be sitting with the Polkinghornes behind him every day at trial, at the beginning of all of this. Why wouldn't I?'

She began to weep.

'Sorry,' I said.

'That's okay.'

'I understand the two of you went to relationship counselling. What was that like?'

'It was all about his obsession and how he can't control it with me. He's obsessed with me.

'How do you think he is now?'

'Pulling off his greatest lie and loving it. Yeah. Absolutely loving it. His greatest act yet.'

'Do you think he misses you?'

'You mean the idea of me? Absolutely. Not the actual me. But I seem to give him his most potent hard-on ever. That was pretty evident.'

'Why do you think he adored you so much?'

'Everyone adores me sexually. I fit a mould, you know. Even without all the cosmetic work, I've always been, when I walk into a room, I am irritatingly sexually attractive. Pretty much everyone in the room, every room I've ever walked in, all over the planet.'

But no one noticed her at the Park Hyatt. Everyone was turned on by the greater stimulant and lubricant of the Melbourne Cup; while we raked over the embers of a murder trial, corks popped, and glasses were being raised all around the room. We were a little corner of unhappiness.

---

We plunged deeper into the unhappy past when she admitted that she had got addicted to methamphetamine. I asked how bad it got, and she said, 'It doesn't take very long to take hold. Yeah. Because you think you're really winning and you're getting ahead, and you are. House is clean. Go to the gym. Make-up is good. Do a photo shoot. Do all your bookings. Like you're just a machine. You're just a product. Produce, produce, produce, produce, produce.'

The waiter took our plates away — mine was licked clean, her soup still contained enough to feed a family of eight — and we ordered two more drinks. Tables of Melbourne Cup fever headed outside, in the sun and closer to the water; the restaurant had emptied. I asked her again how she thought Polkinghorne would be coping, and she seized on the news story that week, broken by Carolyne Meng-Yee, that he had been erased from the Northern Club, that beautiful hitching post for the rich, just up the road from the High Court.

She said, 'It's a big slap in the face. He'll be hurt by that.'

I pondered the second act of Polkinghorne's life, how there had been a Polkinghorne before Pauline's death and a Polkinghorne afterwards, and I saw them as different creatures — one an anonymous surgeon happily living his best late-life crisis life, the other on the run from his existence as a pariah, a living legend wanting to keep his head down. I said to her, 'Surely he's going to stay clean, stay out of trouble.'

She said, 'You can't teach him anything. He's impervious.'

The longer the interview continued, the more she lashed out, not just at Polkinghorne, but pretty much everyone: Ruth, Pauline, Tracey, the detectives who worked the case. But it made me wonder what was behind it. I got the feeling of someone lonely and isolated. I said to her, 'I was really saddened when you said you didn't have friends. Did you mean that?'

She said, 'I just have to accept it. And if it's not because of my occupation, it's because people get envious about my appearance or the power of my appearance, and perceive that it's not deserved, not earned. So it's basically the curse of being considered a beautiful woman. It's just always there and it's just particularly unfair.

'I've had so much trauma, like, acute trauma. I actually don't want to have relationships. I just want to have a relationship with me and enjoy my money in a really nice way.'

'Well, what about fellow sex workers? They must understand; they'd get it, right?'

'They're worse,' she said. 'Much worse. Envy, competitiveness. And I'm tired of their behaviour as well. You know, they don't act like businesses. I can't relate to them. I want to talk about profit and loss and overheads and tax minimisation. But they don't pay tax. And yesterday I was at the New Zealand Sex Workers' Collective with Catherine Healy.'

Healy is the collective's national co-ordinator. I asked, 'And how was that?'

'Hated it,' she said. 'Never want to see her again. She's really nice, by the way. But nice doesn't cut it for me anymore.'

'What did you hate?'

'She never once contacted me. They never published anything on their social media about it because they're a weak organisation that gives out condoms. You know what? I'll buy my own, thanks.'

She talked about wanting the collective to put pressure on Crown prosecution to make it one of Polkinghorne's bail terms that he could not engage with sex workers. An international porn star and escort claimed in an interview with Carolyne Meng-Yee that Polkinghorne contacted her two days after Pauline died, and they met for sex in June ($3000 for two hours); another sex worker claimed he booked her in July ($5000) and later joined him for a fortnight at the Coromandel beach house. The first sex worker was referred to in the story as a friend of Madison.

'She's not my mate. She was never a friend. A lot of sex workers are fixated on me. They've got nothing better to do. They're not the smartest bunch, you know, like they are physically gorgeous, but they don't imbue themselves with, you know, business ethics or seek out skills to sort of solidify and formalise their routine.'

I said, 'So how do you approach the business? Is it like entrepreneurial capitalism?'

'No, it's small business capitalism. I'm a trust that owns the company. I get paid a wage and that's about it. I just funnel it all to superannuation.'

'Are you running a good business?'

'Yeah,' she said. 'I'm a dead-easy sell. I've got great, really great loyal customers. Conducting a relationship for a lot of people is out of their price point. They can't. It's just not feasible. So I guess I sort of fall into the booking of a regular girl. I turn up on time and just get on with it. You know, I'm like, "Just relax and have a really good afternoon or whatever."

'And it's the accrued savings and the compound interest on your investments that are the things that really, really, really matter. So it's living well below your overheads and all that sort of stuff.'

She claimed her annual income before tax was $750,000.

---

My girlfriend joined us for a drink. They kissed each other on the cheek, and Madison said, 'I like your tattoo.' It was as though the sun had come out: it was the first nice thing she had said about anybody, an actual compliment, given warmly and happily. My partner asked if she had any tattoos, and Madison went into some detail about wanting a tattoo around her stomach of her favourite porn stars.

Her compliment was also the last nice thing she said about anybody. Relaxed by the second beer, the good cheer of the Melbourne Cup, and my partner's beauty and grace, I mentioned in passing that even if she had turned up at the High Court to give evidence, the prosecution may only have led with her evidence for an hour. She was horrified. Her bitterness returned. I asked her, 'Do you think you actually would have made a difference?'

She said, 'Oh my God. Obviously, obviously. But no one in that room cared about me, and I'm supposed to go in there and save the day, but if they're not asking me serious questions, then there's no point in me being there. They didn't even acknowledge my relationship. They fucking shot themselves in the foot. I would have been an absolute *weapon*. Had they just saved me from him and told me he was married — the whole thing really starts and ends with that.'

She said she would have needed to have been in the witness box for at least two days to have told her story. But her evidence about his methamphetamine use, and the lies she claimed he told her about living apart from Pauline and wanting to set up home with her, could have been dealt with fairly quickly. Little else would have been of any use to the Crown. Even more unrealistically, she said she wouldn't have put up with being cross-examined by Ron Mansfield.

None of it ever came to pass. Her appearance in Auckland came two months too late and it was only to talk to the media. A documentary, a podcast, a book — none of it served any purpose in bringing Polkinghorne to the justice she felt was still due. All it amounted to was sitting with a writer in the Park Hyatt and talking about how no one in the police or prosecution gave her what she craved, and certainly what she deserved: respect.

'It's like, once all this, all this product is wrapped up and I'm walking away, you know, I don't want to do any more interviews about this. I just want to dump it.'

'When are you going to do your last interview?'

'This might be it. I think this is it. This is it.'

There was no one else left in the restaurant. Staff repeatedly told us that last drinks had already been called. They wanted us to leave, and finish cleaning up. We stayed where we were, and she said, 'I loved those lines you had about Philip. "Odious sex midget." That was hilarious.'

'Thank you.'

'That was a good one. Was that the first line like that?'

'No, the first one was "malignant sex dwarf".'

'I think I was in London by that stage,' she said, meaning her escape from appearing at the High Court.

'How was that trip? Was it weird, reading about the trial while everyone was looking for you?'

'It was surreal. I mean, good surreal. I was mainlining on it, you know, while having my ass handed to a whole country in another time zone. I would go out for some of the days, but there was a few days where I just couldn't get out of bed. Like, you know, some of the prosecution stuff about me. What was her name? The prosecutor?'

'Alysha McClintock. It was you who emailed her the photos of Philip in a Santa hat at your place, wasn't it?'

'Yeah. Did she mention that to you?'

'She said she received them from an email address she didn't recognise, or something like that.'

'Well, did she use it as evidence?'

'It's not really something you can produce as evidence,' I said.

'But it's got the geomarker. I sent it with the geomarker. What's wrong with these people? You don't need me there for that. They have the photo. There's the geomarker. Oh, my God. So I was hoping to meet her this week. Alysha. I'll try. Because she fucking owes me an apology. She denigrated my character over and over and over. And, you know, like, they never, ever painted me as I am, which was an abused partner. I want her to apologise and I'll give her every opportunity this week to do so. Who the fuck do they think they are?'

I asked, 'You're gonna shoot her an email or something?'

'No, I'm just gonna turn up to their office. They'd just ignore my emails. They're not gonna take me seriously if I don't turn up, and it's only around the corner from where I'm staying.'

The door to the restaurant was gigantic, a mass of timber fashioned like a barn door. A waiter closed it by pulling on a chain. It took quite a while for the door to slide across and the whole operation was extremely loud and an extremely clear sign for us to please just leave. It was kind of embarrassing. It was amateur hour. It was petty New Zealand at its worst, the country that loves nothing more than closing down. It was the New Zealand that Madison Ashton loathed.

We packed up to leave. I gabbled, 'How was it being in

Auckland? I just mean being in the scene of the crime, so to speak. I mean where Pauline died. The house.'

'Like I never want to be back ever,' she said. 'I'll just see out the next few days, finish it all off, and they'll have enough content to do their projects, and I'll just, you know, be back home in the weekend with the dogs. And that's it. Out of here.'

We stood up and exchanged kisses on the cheek.

She said, 'You know what I regret? Not physically having a crack at him, like with a wire brush or something. Like I really regret not getting it out of my system. He'd have screamed like a stuck hog.'

'What would you have done? Whacked him on the head or something?'

'Blinded him,' she said. 'Actually that's the dream I had for several months, every day. It was crazy.'

'Blinding the eye doctor.'

'Yeah.'

'What was the vision in your dream?'

'That his eyes were boiling out. And it was so real. It was freaking me out, like really freaking me out.'

'Was it like a daytime fantasy or in your dreams?'

'In my sleep. Yeah. And I wake up going, "It's done."'

We parted ways. My girlfriend said I should have invited her somewhere else for a drink. It was such a lovely afternoon. Outside, the Melbourne Cuppers were hooraying and hurrahing, tipsy in the sun. I wished I had asked her. She was so witty, with a quick mind that came up with strange words ('porous', 'ne'er do wells'). She was fun company, a lovely, lonely, damaged, successful and intelligent woman from across the sea who got caught up in the crime of the New Zealand century, was close to its principal character, may even have been in love with him, and came to view him as one of the most dangerous men alive. The last question I asked her was, 'Was that okay? How are you feeling?'

'Tired,' she said.

CHAPTER 11

# A Night at the Opera

It ended without an ending. By the last week of the trial, the hands on the university clock tower were finally showing the right time; spring was springing reds, yellows and greens out of the trees surrounding Old Government House; the natural order of things was only lacking at the High Court of Auckland, with its inability not just to convict but also to exonerate. The jury's note to the judge made it clear they thought the evidence was lacking for murder and was also lacking for suicide. 'This case is binary. If it's not suicide, it's murder,' Crown prosecutor Alysha McClintock told the jury in her magnificent two-day closing address. Magnificent, in tone and logic and narrative, in prose better than most crime fiction; magnificent, too, in its grand opera; its presentation of ruling passions; its tragic staging. And yet it was a massive failure. It was thought of as unconvincing, unbelievable. The root of its problem was the binary dilemma. McClintock was wrong. There was no clear choice. If it's not suicide, it doesn't follow that it's murder. There was no proof for either death. The jury blocked off the exits. Not suicide, not murder; not guilty, the whole thing trailing off into a mystery that will last forever.

One day during proceedings I escaped courtroom 11 — Ron Mansfield was boring everyone to tears with a long cross-examination of an IT expert who looked like Ringo — and took my thermos of instant coffee and my supplies of pretzels and raisins to the High Court basement, to move among the perfect silences of the Law Society library. I wanted to get away from the trial of the century and wander the hallways of another century; the library was stocked with volumes dealing in ancient troubles, and I chose a history of English law in the eleventh and twelfth centuries. One passage dealt with standards of proof. They were not especially intellectually robust standards: 'Many of these methods were primitive, oracular, like interrogations of supernatural forces or beings . . . *The Domesday Book* shows a number of ordeals of hot iron.' That actually sounded preferable to what was going on upstairs — or rather, what was *not* going on, and not just with Ringo but with the entire civilised apparatus of the Polkinghorne trial, its necessary cautions, its ponderous analyses. Because it got nowhere. It literally didn't prove anything. It might have achieved a result, any result, if they had brought out the hot iron. It might have come to more rational conclusions, any conclusions, had they interrogated phantoms, deities, ectoplasms. All possibilities must be explored. The truth was out there in plain sight over those eight weeks, disassembled and scattered, argued and complicated, picked up and put down somewhere else, no stone left unturned and then turned back — the grand opera of the Polkinghorne trial ended in a grand meaninglessness.

But the sound and fury of its closing addresses signified more than nothing. Both of them contained versions of the truth. It was out there in the two days that McClintock spoke and the two days that Mansfield spoke. They were like competing operas, the only form that was appropriate to the Polkinghorne trial. I received quite a few emails during the trial imploring me to turn it into a musical. I thought that was in poor taste, and that's rich coming from me. The trial was too serious, too tragic, too intense for anything as light-hearted or facile as a stage musical; opera, however, gets to its noise and spectacle, its love triangle ending in death. The Crown banged a loud drum of guilt as Alysha McClintock picked up the tiny figure of Polkinghorne and paraded him through courtroom 11 in the classic operatic role of a rich man who killed his wife to be with the woman of his erotic dreams: Madison Ashton, in this scenario, playing the classic operatic role of the high-class courtesan. It was a version of Verdi's great work *La Traviata*, about a courtesan who sells herself to the debauched ruling class: 'Nothing in the world matters except pleasure!' It was a riff, too, on *Pretty Woman*, the film adaptation of *La Traviata*, with Madison Ashton as a passable Julia Roberts, hooker who meets old rich guy. Not that Polkinghorne could ever pass for Richard Gere, but life and movie ran parallel in that client and provider fell in something resembling love.

McClintock's aria was as black as her robe, as black as the curtains pulled across the windows of courtroom 11. There was a change in routine to court procedure. Rest breaks were allowed each hour as McClintock sang of Polkinghorne's venality to her audience of 11 jurors. Her address formed a libretto in three acts.

## ACT 1

An opening act of a tragic opera presents a problem, suggests conflict, foreshadows the dread finger of fate up to no good. McClintock introduced the characters and walked it back, starting from the events of 5 April 2021. Always, she stayed close to the death, its before and after; she was to save the actual death until Act 3.

Brian Dickey was due to give the closing address. The trial went longer than anticipated and he had to depart to take a slow boat around the Baltic. It ate at him; he was really looking forward to closing. It would have been his swansong, his final act in his 'one last case' on his temporary comeback to the Crown desk, and I have no doubt he would have thrown himself into it, yelled, seethed, made it dark and terrifying and hateful. But I don't know if it would have been any improvement on Alysha McClintock, who did all those things with amazing precision. She gave the best closing address I have ever heard her deliver, one of the best I have ever heard anywhere. The sentences were strong and supple. They were not one word too long. They were close to crime noir's hard-boiled prose, to match the dark shadows she threw in her re-creation of the mean streets of Remuera.

Act 1 as follows is in her words.

'When the police walked up the steps on the morning of the fifth of April 2021, into the house of Dr Philip Polkinghorne and Pauline Hanna, they assumed that the man who stood in front of them was the devastated husband and that the woman laid out on the floor in that position was his wife, Pauline Hanna.

'The police going into that house, as they normally do, looked around to assess the suicide. And they looked at the supposed hanging mechanism. The rope. It was secured to the balustrade. So they tested that rope, not expecting what happened next to happen, which was that under minimal tension it simply fell to the ground.

'The police decided to explore the possibility that Dr Polkinghorne, renowned eye surgeon, man of wealth and standing, had killed his wife and staged it as a suicide. He may have thought he could talk his way out of it. He is highly intelligent. He certainly sees himself as smart. There is an arrogance to Dr Polkinghorne that I suggest you should not underestimate. And he may have thought the police wanted to rubberstamp Pauline's suicide.

'Pauline Hanna's death at first pass did look like a suicide. It was meant to. But Pauline didn't hang herself. The Crown case is that he has taken his wife's life, and he has blamed her for it. As he blamed her in life, he blames her in death. This case is binary. If it's not suicide, it's murder. Pauline Hanna did not die by accident. She did not die by disease. She did not die by mistake. If it isn't suicide, it's murder.

'This evidence clearly portrays a man that doesn't fit with a man devastated by his wife's suicide. Firstly, he erased evidence. Secondly, he secretly tried to access whether he had left a clue on his wife's dead body. Thirdly, he started to try and manipulate those who knew Pauline and tried to paint her as suicidal.

'His priority, having made some calls about his wife's death, was to delete his WhatsApp messages, including his entire conversation history with Madison Ashton dating back to 2017. During the police interview, Polkinghorne left the room for a break at 4.28 p.m. and when Detective Andrew Reeves examined the doctor's phone later, he found no WhatsApp messages before April 5, at about 4.30 p.m. None of his messaging before then is available, but we know they'd been in regular contact before that, and a further review of his phone found he used it multiple times overnight between April 4 and 5, when he told police he was asleep.

'Wouldn't you like to know what was being said between those two before April 5? But you don't, because Dr Polkinghorne has manipulated the evidence and deleted them. The clear and obvious and I would say *only* inference as to why he did this at that point in time at the police station is because they contained messages demonstrating that he was not the devastated husband at all.

'The next search that he does and deletes is hugely significant, and it comes on the sixth of April. This search unmasks the murderer, I suggest. "Leg oedema after strangulation." *After* strangulation. In this context, it conveys murder rather than conveying suicide. The one and only explanation is he's trying to check if he had left behind a clue. He understands the working of the body and was worried that he'd left a trace.

'Thirdly, he went around to his friend Paul Adriaanse's house and encouraged him not to speak to police. Then there's Alison Ring, Pauline Hannah's good friend. Polkinghorne went around to her house and started speaking ill of his wife, and also procured a suicide note he said he'd found in her bedding. He knew, as Alison Ring told you, that Pauline Hanna always left notes for everything. He knew questions were being asked about why she hadn't left a note. He is trying to manipulate Alison Ring. And as she told you, that's exactly how she saw it. "I felt I had been manipulated by him." That's what she told you.

'Remember what he's telling us in the days, weeks and months that follow her death is that he's devastated. Devastated, he says. I suggest you would be right, members of the jury, to resist his claims of devastation. It's very telling that just three weeks after the loss of his wife to a supposed suicide, he was off on a holiday to a remote part of the country with Madison Ashton. Either he and his devastation just happened to have found comfort in the arms of Madison Ashton in the South Island, or this is what he wanted when he decided, either that his wife was in the way and he strangled her, or whether he did that more spontaneously during an argument. Could be either of those things. But this is the life he wanted.'

I thought Act 1 of Ron Mansfield's opening address was one of the worst I have ever heard. I felt it ambled and rambled, and not content with that hot air, it preambled. It was the improvisation of a jazz bore who played all the notes, noodling on the sax of his flat nasal honking voice; his sentences were long and loose and flabby, without discipline or dynamic. Sometimes, though, he tried to locate heart-wrenching melodies. His voice shook with staged grief at the 'insults and indignities' suffered by Polkinghorne. He spoke at immense volume. He stood with his hands in his pockets. Jurors now and then met his eye. Some gazed at the windows with real longing.

If the prosecution turned the trial into a version of *La Traviata*, Mansfield preferred *Madama Butterfly*, i.e. the heroine dies by suicide. But the only character he introduced in Act 1 was Polkinghorne. He asked the jury to feel sorry for him. What a pointless exercise. All the sympathy in the room lay at all times with Pauline.

Act 1 as follows is in his own words.

'Your Honour, Mister Foreman and members of your jury. What a final insult. The final insult Dr Polkinghorne faces from 5 April, 2021 through to today's date has just been made by the Crown. It suggested that he's blamed her, his own wife, for her death. He's described as the master manipulator. The first insult he faced was when the police attended at his address on 5 April, 2021, when they walk through that door with our open mind, or so they would have us believe, and then very quickly saw the rope in the way in which it was left by Dr Polkinghorne and gave it what they describe as the tension check, and from there he was treated in a way that he was alleged to have been involved in his wife's own death. It was an insult because what lay behind that was the suspicion they never informed him of or gave him the opportunity to respond to then and there, despite grieving the death of his wife.

'Dr Polkinghorne agreed to be interviewed at the scene when he detailed quite consistently what happened that morning. A master manipulator need not have done so, but he did so in the state that he was in inbetween taking messages, making calls, letting people know, as any one of us would like the dignity to do, to let people know who loved Pauline of her passing, to allow people to comfort you as you might when you suffer such a loss. But nonetheless, during that interview, we know this tension check took place, and we know things switched from an open mind and being objective by the attending police officers to a focus now on establishing what they were quickly coming to think was a potential homicide.

'They failed to tell him that they considered the situation to be suspicious and that he might be a suspect for his own wife's death. They lured him to the police station, albeit under a false pretence that they wanted an interview, not from a grieving husband who might find it cathartic to sit there and talk about his wife and what he had found in the way in which it appeared during the course of the interview he found it, but treating him like a suspect for his own wife's death.

'Dr Polkinghorne had no idea during his lengthy police interview that a forensic team and a photographer had been set loose in his house. It was another insult given he had been speaking with the police openly and honestly to find his home was being violated and he was being treated as a suspect. The deleted WhatsApp messages came after the revelation that he was being treated as a suspect. When you think about the timing of that, and given the level of suspicion he was facing and the focus of the police investigation, why would he want the police to learn of something that was private between him and his wife in relation to what they or what he got up to by way of sexual relations outside of their union. It is entirely understandable at that point why he might seek to delete or remove WhatsApp messages that revealed something which was intimate and potentially embarrassing, and certainly something that would damage both of their reputations.

'The police sealed off the Upland Road home from April fifth to April 16. Pauline's funeral was on April 15, and Dr Polkinghorne had to investigate purchasing new clothes for fear he wouldn't be able to get any of her personal effects from the address. Tongues were wagging around Remuera because of the presence of the police, and soon the press was onto it and people soon came to know the death was being treated as suspicious. When this became public that the death was being treated as suspicious and he was the suspect, then everyone around him starts to shut down, treats him differently, and he becomes isolated.

'It made people think differently when it eventually came time for them to be interviewed by police. Things that might have otherwise been seen as drunken banter that they didn't place much weight on then, now became quite important. Their attitudes and experiences were informed by the fact that Dr Polkinghorne was suspected by police of killing his wife. People's views changed in a flick of a switch.

'The only person who was engaging with him was Madison Ashton, with whom he had been in a relationship with for six years since 2015. As a result of this and police investigation and the way in which they are conducting it, he has become entirely isolated. And yeah, there's sexual discussion and sexual engagement entirely consistent with the nature of their relationship for that entire period from 2015, that entire period that both he and Pauline have known this woman and utilised her services and support. And given that she's the only person that's reaching out to him, that's communicating with him, it is hardly surprising that their relationship draws close. And so Dr Polkinghorne's meeting with Madison Ashton in Mount Cook Village 25 days after Pauline's death can be understood.'

## ACT 2

I felt Mansfield's second act was even worse. Act 2 in classic opera builds on conflict, a problem made real and then acute; in Mansfield's telling, the problem was Pauline's mental state. Now and then he cast her as a woman in distress. He presented the Polkinghornes as a happy couple enjoying an open marriage; the only problem was Pauline, with her drinking, her medication, her stress, her history of anxiety. He made a powerful case, but he wandered from it, almost at will. His aria lacked shape, it felt like a randomly selected set of issues, it argued every small detail into the ground. There were strange and unsatisfactory zingers, as when he accused Alysha McClintock of impersonating TV star Angela Lansbury. You could feel he regretted it as soon as he tried it on.

I exchanged texts with another reporter in court. 'Ron's first hour was complete horseshit,' I wrote. 'It really was eh,' came the reply. 'Car boot lawyer stuff.' I liked that line and plagiarised it in a text I sent to a criminal defence lawyer, who I regularly updated on the trial. They replied, 'Oh no! Has Ron fallen at the final hurdle?'

It really felt like it. Mansfield reached a nadir when he tried to dismiss the 37-gram stash of methamphetamine as no big deal. Maybe, he suggested, Polkinghorne bought it in bulk, and it was 'just sitting around the house'. No problem. 'No relevance.' No kidding. I texted, 'This is such bullshit. "The meth was just lying around." Jesus.' Reply from my colleague on the press bench: 'He's on a hiding to nothing here. Polky gonna fry.' I answered, '8 weeks and all he has is this phoney bullshit. Jury over it.' I was over it and bleakly considered taking a break to sit in on the only other proceeding at the High Court that day — *Refrigerant Recovery NZ Ltd v The Trust for the Destruction of Synthetic Refrigerants.*

Act 2 as follows is in Mansfield's words.

'Pauline was vulnerable and had vulnerabilities. All the evidence clearly establishes that Pauline died by suicide. There is no justice for Pauline if you ignore her vulnerabilities and do not respect the decision she took. The decision you make must be on the evidence, that is the oath that you swore. It can't be based on emotion, and it can't be based on a foundless theory that he wanted her out of his life and he was prepared to kill her, for which there is no forensic evidence to support. Hold him morally to account if need be, as he has been in this very public way. But you cannot convict a man of murder when they did not do it. That is not following your oath. It is just being emotional vigilantes.

'The answer has always been in the pathology. The answer is still in the pathology. And the answer doesn't justify how long his address was under the control of the police so that they could search it in the way that they did. The answer doesn't justify the very long way he had to wait until he found out that he was going to be accused of his wife's death, and it doesn't answer why we're here today. They had to justify it through some other means by seeking to build a motive for a murder that has simply not been committed.

'That is why we have been here weeks exploring potential motives for a crime that has not been committed, for a murder that has not occurred. And that is why, and that is the only reason why. Because of the absence of forensic evidence from the scene, the absence of any other evidence that you would ordinarily find associated with a homicide. This is some of the gravest nonsense New Zealand courts had heard for a long time.

'A trial run by emotion allows our murder mystery fantasies to run wild. And what a blockbuster my learned friend's closing address was. It was like a binge of every *Murder, She Wrote*, by our own, our very own Angela Lansbury.

'There were no injuries on Pauline from her fighting for her life, none of the scratches or bruises that can occur as she fought back. Of the four pathologists heard in the case, only two had examples of this phantom theory of a death by way of homicidal strangulation but leaving no injury at all. We have unmasked the phantom, folks apparently, and it's Dr Polkinghorne. Dr Polkinghorne, without any training in martial arts, without being a big or strong man, managed to kill his wife without leaving any of the telltale signs.

'The Crown, once it realised that the absence of those kinds of injuries was a real problem for its case, started going rogue. Their framing of Dr Polkinghorne as the master manipulator is designed to turn the jury off him. His entire lifestyle has been laid bare before you, unnecessarily I would say, simply to create the villain that the Crown want you to see him as. Dr Polkinghorne had a number of faults and some of you may see his traits or conduct as something you might not like in a friend or partner. But this is not a court of morals. That includes not judging his meth use or his use of sex workers.

'The evidence shows that Pauline was involved at the outset of the relationship between Dr Polkinghorne and Madison Ashton in 2015, and she spoke of his use of sex workers in the Longlands recording. This is how Pauline and Dr Polkinghorne chose to live their life. Messages from the end of 2020 and early 2021 show that they still loved and supported each other despite how they operated their relationship, and there's no evidence that Dr Polkinghorne wanted to run off with Madison Ashton. That changed after Pauline's death when he was isolated and desperate.

'Dr Polkinghorne developed an interest in the lives of sex workers and the fact he helped them with personal and financial issues says a great deal about him. But ultimately, the use of sex workers may have been another factor that led to Pauline Hanna seeking to take her own life. That he was seeing a well-known sex worker in Australia might have impacted on her decision to take her own life that morning. The problem with the Crown theory regarding his relationship with sex workers equally applies to providing another risk factor for Pauline that might have meant that she saw suicide as a decision for her that morning.

'The Crown relies on a number of actions they say were inconsistent with a grieving husband, such as the search for leg oedema after strangulation. But Dr Polkinghorne wanted to know why the death was still being considered suspicious. There is nothing indicative of this search unmasking the murderer. That is just scare tactics and frankly quite bizarre. He is not simply conducting a search checking to see whether he left behind a clue. What he's endeavouring to do is to find out why it's thought that his wife's death was suspicious and whether the swelling he's noted in her leg might be indicative of that concern.

'Dr Polkinghorne is not a perfect man. None of us would like all our messages trawled through, our internet searches, reviewed by others, or our personal lives turned upside down in the way in which his life and his wife's life was turned upside down as a necessity because of this allegation. None of us could stand there and say we are perfect. There would always be things we wouldn't want others to know, and there would always be things that we would want to keep to ourselves and not be judged for.

'Despite what people think about his interest with sex workers and fascination with pornography, Dr Polkinghorne loved Pauline Hanna and she loved him.'

---

Alysha McClintock's closing address was scheduled to begin at the earlier time of 9.30 a.m. — court usually sits from 10 a.m. The ten-minute breaks each hour further put the trial out of whack with other cases heard in the High Court, and I used one of the breaks to sit in on another murder trial, in a smaller courtroom. Like the Polkinghorne case, it centred on an incident in Remuera, but at a less salubrious address — the Remuera Motor Lodge and Campground, $130 per night, caravan sites available. I called into the sentencing. The accused had changed his plea to guilty. He stabbed a man in the head, neck and back. He informed the court that he believed he was a direct descendant of King

Arthur, Mary and Jesus. He sat in court wearing a little blue yarmulke on top of his wild-haired head. He was duly given a hybrid sentence of eight years in prison and at the Mason Clinic. Who among us can relate to any of that tale of ordinary madness? It was a reminder that many trials concern the actions of the poor and marginalised. The Polkinghornes were executive class, but understandable to anyone in any kind of white-collar work, with their office lives, their busy schedules, their after-work rituals of pinot and Netflix, their overwhelming whiteness. For all of Polkinghorne's use of hookers and SWEET PUFF, he was just another married Auckland householder. Certainly, there was some resemblance between Polkinghorne and that amazing feature of the High Court — the amazing gargoyles sculpted by Anton Teutenberg in the 1860s, their faces leering and moaning above the gutters, visible to all who approach. But McClintock resisted the temptation to demonise him, to present him as monstrous. Her version of Polkinghorne was closer to the famous lines of W.H. Auden:

> Evil is unspectacular and always human,
> And shares our bed and eats at our own table . . .

Her second act was even better than the first. It stayed close to the need to build on conflict; in McClintock's telling, the problem was Polkinghorne's secret life, his dream of everlasting carnal happiness with Madison Ashton. She made a powerful case, and she did so with steely resolve. Throughout, she repeatedly appealed for common sense, and its absence thereof in Polkinghorne's defence that his wife died by suicide. 'It makes no sense,' she said.

'It doesn't make any sense . . . Does this make sense? . . . It makes no sense.' In case there was any doubt, she held the sides of her lectern, leaned forward, and said, 'It. Doesn't. Make. Any. Sense.'

Act 2 is in her own words.

'We are dealing, members of the jury, with a very unusual case and a very complex defendant. He is a man with high levels of intelligence and self-assurance. He appeared to be living a very comfortable life with his wife of 20 years. He was a renowned professional. He was all of those things, it seems, but he was also living another life. Evidence shows he was a man spending hundreds of thousands of dollars on sex workers and drugs to try and keep his secret life away from Pauline. He was living in another world, a world increasingly centred around Madison Ashton and their relationship which at least in his mind, was his future. This dream life that he had with Madison Ashton could not be reconciled with the life he had at home with Pauline Hanna. It was a collision of these two worlds.

'Pauline Hanna was not a woman who had given up. She was a woman whose husband had given up on her. Pauline was a beautiful, successful woman in her early sixties. She loved her family and treated Dr Polkinghorne's children as her own. She could suffer a crisis of confidence from time to time, especially in her work during the COVID pandemic, but she was flourishing in her job at the time of her death and looking forward to the opening of a new vaccination centre.

'Pauline was sad but philosophical about her mother's death and had come to terms with it. She was on Prozac for 20 years but was taking a standard dose. Her blood alcohol limit at the time of death was below the legal limit. And she did not attempt suicide between 1990 and 1992, as alleged by her sister Tracey Hanna in evidence. This was a great shocking piece of information, and yet Tracey also told you she kept it buried in the recesses of her memory for something close to 30 years. I can't explain Tracey Hanna's motivation to say what she did about Pauline, whether it's driven by jealousy of Pauline, by some sort of odd fascination with Dr Polkinghorne, by a wish to be a centre of attention, who knows, but I suggest it is unsafe to rely upon.

'Dr Polkinghorne was both Pauline's greatest love and her greatest vulnerability. He was the husband who she called an angry, angry man in that Longlands recording when things didn't go his way. The husband she knew would have sex with sex workers in Sydney, but who she didn't want doing so on her patch, and she said that she was clear about that. The husband who expected sex from her every day and would go into her bedroom demanding it. The husband who criticised her, blamed her, told her not to wear bodysuits. He was the husband who had strangled her and threatened her that he could do it anytime. He was the husband, though, that she loved despite all of it. The Crown does not and has not contested that she loved him. It's clear that she loved him. She loved him dearly. She kept trying to better herself to make him happy. The great tragedy of all of those is that her love for Dr Polkinghorne ultimately cost her life.

'Pauline had her life together despite her struggles. But she turns up dead under a sheet at the bottom of the stairs, totally out of the blue and a shock to all of those close to her.

'If you follow the suicide narrative, she chooses the front doorway, in the most public part of the house, where she will be seen by whoever enters that doorway. She's naked but for a dressing gown in the most public part of the house, naked under a loose dressing gown, this hugely proud, immaculate woman who impulsively decided to leave this world pretty much naked.

'If you follow the suicide narrative, Pauline got up at some point in the night despite the high levels of Zopiclone in her system, but she didn't touch her phone or her laptop. She also didn't go to the toilet, despite having a full bladder when she died. Instead, she made a mess of a room, stripped just the top sheet off the bed, and took off the pillowcases, which appeared to have vanished. Pauline then went naked apart from her robe to get the rope, but we don't know exactly where from. If it's still in the ute, then she went outside, with a full bladder, in her robe undone, to get it. She would have had to cut the rope but then hidden the cutting implement in her disinhibited state. She then would have had to truss one bit of rope to the balustrade without any search on her phone and laptop before moving a chair into the hallway. She also fetched a leather belt to attach to the rope, despite her robe having a belt. She would have done all of this without being noticed by Dr Polkinghorne, who we know was using his laptop until around 2.40 a.m.

'The very first piece of evidence the jury heard was the 111 call at 8:07 a.m. when Dr Polkinghorne said he'd found his wife. From the point the operator told him to cut Pauline down, he would have had to remove her from the chair she was sitting on, undo the rope and belt, and then lay her down on the ground and then check if she was breathing. That's a lot to do, especially when he says he's in shock. Yet he managed to do it all and in about 10 seconds.'

## ACT 3

During the playing of the 111 call in court, I had marvelled at how quickly it had taken Polkinghorne to cut the rope, then race back to talk to the operator. But I thought nothing more of it and had completely forgotten it until McClintock raised it in her closing address. It felt significant that the jury asked to hear the 111 call again. They surely wanted to test McClintock's theory and count how long it took; everyone in the courtroom surely did the same; I did — and timed it just as McClintock had said: ten seconds. It was revealed as a secret test of Polkinghorne's credibility and strengthened the Crown case that Polkinghorne had staged it as a suicide. I asked her afterwards whether she had saved that brilliant little calculation for the closing. 'God yes,' she said.

Clever. But of course it counted for nowt. It was just another circumstantial stick that the Crown hoped the jury would throw onto a bonfire of guilt. There was no flame. Mansfield's pathologists had doused it with their findings that there was no evidence to support a homicidal death. The death was everything. Motive, drug use, hookers, the before and the after — none of it mattered as much as the death. Act 3 was all about the death, its tragic circumstance, its final and terrible result — and it was where the Crown case suddenly, abruptly, devastatingly failed. It fell at the final hurdle.

Acts 1 and 2 were so certain, so sure, so emphatic for the Crown. But McClintock was reduced to trying to make excuses for the pathology, to sweeping it under the carpet. 'On pathology, the findings here are very limited and not decisive, nor need they be. The findings establish the cause of death as neck compression and not much more, but it is speculative to use the absence of other injuries to support suicide . . . The pathology only takes us so far.' But it wasn't true. The pathology took us all the way, to death's door.

Her own imagining of what happened sounded speculative, vague. Her sentences no longer had the same sense of purpose or confidence. 'Something has happened between them that night . . . We don't know.' Her argument was lost in the shadows.

Act 3 is in her own words.

'He's obsessed with Madison Ashton. He thinks he's setting up a life with her. It's clear in his messages that that's what he thinks. It supports the logical conclusion that Dr Polkinghorne and Pauline argued about something that night, or these issues boiled over for Dr Polkinghorne that night and he made his decision to strangle his wife.

'Dr Christopher Milroy, one of the defence pathologists, acknowledged that while rare, it was possible to strangle someone without leaving significant injuries. And Pauline's injuries are not nonspecific when viewed through a lens of control and aggression. Either she's been surprised in the ensuing struggle, she's been struck and punched and gripped and strangled, or there's an argument during which she's been struck and punched and gripped and strangled. This is about connecting everything together, so it's really important not to get trapped into isolating bits of evidence. You should also remember that Dr Polkinghorne is a doctor and would have been avoiding making it look like he killed his wife.

'Onto the night itself, Dr Polkinghorne lied to police about going to bed at 10 p.m. The data shows his phone is active after that, including him putting it on airplane mode between 1:11 a.m. and 8:06 a.m. He still used his phone during that time. He is active for much of this night. And the point is he had plenty of time to kill her. He had plenty of time to get himself in a state about Madison Ashton, plenty of time to have a toot on SWEET PUFF, plenty of time to either surprise his wife in her bedroom or argue with her and strangle her there or somewhere else. You don't have to be sure about where but the upstairs bedroom does seem the most likely place. Plenty of time for his wife to at least leave one mark on him as she tried to fight back, that cut to his head that he simply couldn't and didn't explain in either his first written statement to the police or his police interview.

'Something has happened between them that night. Maybe he is high and strung out on meth. We don't know. But in simple terms, his wife has died on a night when it is clear he is awake much of that night, and he has inexplicably put his phone on airplane mode and he has had time to do all of these things.

'He had the intelligence to do it. He had the arrogance, the meth-fuelled courage. His relationship with Pauline Hanna was done. He had detached from that life. He blamed Pauline Hanna in life and it is the final insult to her to blame her for her own death. I suggest, members of the jury, that the evidence that you have heard proves the lie that Dr Polkinghorne told when he phoned 111 and said that she had hung herself. I suggest you can safely be sure on this evidence that he's guilty of murder.'

Act 3 belonged to Mansfield. He dropped the improvising and stuck to a script; he wrote the end of his closing address and delivered it in tough little sentences that sounded like fact. The surer he sounded, the louder he spoke. This is how it ended, how this tabloid hack wanted it to end: not with a bang, nothing lowercase about it, but with a roisterous, whooping BANG. He shouted, he hollered, he very nearly screamed. He was one man on his feet yelling in a full courtroom.

I thought it was magnificent, the proper and right way to end a trial as immense as the grand opera season of Polkinghorne, and after he sat down, exhausted, and the deafened jury left for tea and yet more Krispies, I shook his hand in congratulations. He seemed only dimly aware. He was spent. He had nothing more to give.

'He loved her!' Mansfield roared at the jury. 'You cannot convict a man of murder when he did not do it! All the evidence clearly confirms that this was death by way of suicide! We all want Justine!' What? Mansfield corrected himself: 'Sorry. We all want justice!'

He said Pauline was stressed, tired, burnt out. He said she was anxious that her husband was seeing someone and would leave her. He said that she mixed wine with sleeping pills but could not sleep. He didn't guess, he didn't speculate; he laid out what happened next in those tough little sentences that read best as single paragraphs. He ended the third and most important act with Pauline's death.

Act 3 is in his own words.

'There is no more lonely place than the early hours of the morning when you can't sleep.

'It is dark.

'It is desperate.

'She got up.

'She got the rope.

'She secured it.

'She tied it to the belt around her neck so she could suspend herself.'

Dark, compelling, powerful; the only problem with it is that it may have been total bullshit.

CHAPTER 12

# Afterwards

Afterwards, nothing; nothing came out of the trial that had everything, that exhausted itself on sex and drugs, that sucked up the fumes of wealth, that fixated on the moods and intentions of a small man in weird socks; nothing happened, nothing changed, nothing could be done about it. The verdict of not guilty left everyone free to go about their business and deal with the vacancy. The cops left looking weak and inefficient. The prosecution left in tears. The defence left feeling in the right. 'We'll win this,' Ron Mansfield had promised Polkinghorne, and part of the strategy was to never let a single Crown witness go unchallenged, to fight them over everything, in a campaign of total war. It was exhausting. But two weeks later, Mansfield was back in the High

Court, defending a man on a charge of attempted murder — the police alleged he strangled his wife.

I interviewed Bruce Hanna about an hour after the verdict. We sat in one of the mean little rooms in the High Court of Auckland where I have interviewed many other families of either the victim or the accused, all of them stunned in some which way by a verdict; Bruce, too, was stunned, had not seen it coming. I asked, 'What do you think of Dr Philip Polkinghorne?' He said, 'He got away with murder.'

I liked Bruce a lot. He was a straight arrow and had the kind of long, friendly farmer's face that would make you spot him in a crowd anywhere in the world as a Kiwi. He couldn't wait to get back to his Hawke's Bay farm, to the dogs. 'To walk the land,' he said. But he admitted he'd come to like Auckland in the two months of the trial. He persisted in coming to court every single day. Every morning, he took his seat in the front row of the public gallery. It was tough for him to go through it and there were times when he slunk back to his hotel room on Beach Road and just lay on the bed, exhausted.

He said in the little High Court room, 'I knew the day he called me at 11.30 in the morning on the fifth of April 2021 that my sister never took her own life. And then the day after that, he phoned me and asked me if I had a copy of Pauline's will, in a quite a normal voice. And I said, "Why the fuck would I have a copy of Pauline's will?"

'He said, "Oh, it's okay. I just wondered." And then hung up. That was like the second conversation I had with him. His wife supposedly took her own life, and I thought, "No way. That's just bullshit."

'And I know my sister. I knew her for sixty years. And I knew that she would not do that without telling me. She would write a note or she would ring me and say she's desperate. So, you know, it's hard to accept, Steve. I always thought the jury would have a hell of a job trying to get their heads around the pathology. But yeah. For the whole three and a half years, I've known he's guilty.'

He will think that for the rest of his days. Weirdly, and fortunately, I doubt it will be with any damaging or permanent bitterness. He has a pragmatism about him. Yet also aspects of him are complex, sensitive. I asked him about Pauline. They were close. 'We laughed a lot,' he said, 'and I still laugh with her now. I still talk to her. Yeah. Still.'

Pauline was 63. The cause of her death was compression of the neck. 'I'm safe, darling,' she told her niece, Bruce's daughter, Rose, at the Longlands dinner party that was recorded and played in court. 'Please think I'm safe.'

Bruce remembered that night. He cooked his speciality, chana masala. Pauline had shocked everyone by telling them about having group sex with her husband and ('Here's the real oil') prostitutes, about how unhappy she was, about how he would get so angry ('on the roof'), that he was out of control, but she loved him, she loved him, she loved him, and he loved her, he loved her, he loved her.

I asked him, 'What do we make of Polkinghorne?'

He said, 'Oh, he is a very clever narcissist. He is a manipulator. He manipulates people for his own advantage. I've seen him doing it for decades.' His family never liked Polkinghorne. They loathed him, for decades. Except for their younger sister, Tracey, with her claim that Pauline had once tried to die by suicide. Bruce said, 'He's clearly sucked in my sister, Tracey, in London and turned her against the family. For her to fly all the way over here, give her evidence in court, not even say hello to us, and walk out and get on a plane and fly back to England — that's his doing.'

Bruce's wife, Shelley, was in the interview room, too, with Rose, and Rose's brother, Jacob. She said, 'Everything that's come about in the trial about Philip — to have got all that detail over eight weeks, it's a huge gift. Because everybody's been sitting there thinking, "What a terrible man." You know, no matter what the verdict is, everyone's saying, "Wow. He's a terrible man."'

Rose said, 'If police had said there's not enough evidence, leave it, you know, let's call it a suicide, none of this would have come out. The extent of Philip's deviousness, and how hard she tried to hold it all together, that she was still trying to hold, you know, to keep her marriage together and try and get him back on track. She really wanted that happy ending.'

I kept wanting to close the interview, leave them to it, especially after they said things with such dreadful finality as, 'She really wanted that happy ending.' But I had nowhere to go. One last lap of the beautiful university gardens, wandering quietly by the yew and the sequoia and the toothed lancewood . . . I was reluctant to leave. I had hung around outside the court for about an hour after the verdict, just leaning against the facade, its stone warming my back. I was about to go when Bruce texted, 'Steve are you still around?' I answered, 'Yeh.' He replied, 'Can you come back inside?' Journalism is actually good for something. It allows people the chance to talk. Bruce and his family had nowhere else to go. The High Court had been like an electrical charge, it was where each day had an edge to it, was getting ever closer to the word and the release the family craved: *Guilty*. Without it, the High Court was now like a shell. Everything had been taken out of it.

'We've still got Pauline's jar of lime marmalade in the fridge,' said Shelley.

Bruce said, 'Is that the Rose's?'

'Yes, the Rose's.'

'Rose's lime marmalade,' I said.

'Yeah. Three years on, it's still sitting there,' said Bruce.

I said, 'I saw it in a supermarket a couple of weeks ago and thought of how Pauline liked it, so I bought a jar.'

'Did you?'

'Yep.'

'Pauline always used to buy that,' said Bruce. 'We thought, "Let's buy our own", because this is Pauline's, and we put it back in the fridge.'

'It's Pauline's,' said Rose.

'And we put a little thing on top. "Pauline's",' said Shelley.

Bruce said, 'That'll stay there forever, probably.'

---

Nothing to do, except drink. I met Crown prosecutor Brian Dickey for a drink at the Cornerbar on Shortland Street after he got back from his cruise-ship holiday in Europe, and he was a long way from being morose about the verdict but nowhere near content, shared a few regrets about the way it was conducted but nothing major, and remained adamant that making the decision to go ahead with a prosecution was the right thing to do, that it needed to be heard before a jury. I met Ron Mansfield for a drink at Little Culprit on Wyndham Street a few weeks later. He was still fairly exhausted from the whole thing and marvelled at how nothing in his career compared to that trial, and when I asked whether, in his heart of hearts, if he had such a thing, whether he believed Polkinghorne had not killed his wife, he was very quick and very direct to state that he absolutely believed he had not, that the suspicion and the arrest and putting him on trial was a travesty.

There was one more drink to be had. It was at the highest bar in New Zealand, tottering 182 metres above the Earth: the SkyBar at the top of the Sky Tower, for the strangest Christmas drinks function in Auckland — a reunion of the Polkinghorne court watchers, the regulars who packed courtroom 11 for eight weeks. They call themselves The Polkinghorne Group. They made up a party of about twenty, drinking champagne and nibbling on fries in a crowded, bustling, noisy bar with 360-degree views of the Auckland isthmus. I gravitated to the hardcore, the ones who took it seriously and treated it like a job, appearing pretty much every day: Lois Osborne, who divides her time between homes in Whangārei and Ponsonby; Jan Naish-Wallis of Howick and Robbyn Storey of Raglan. It was nice to see them and even though it was difficult to reconcile their festive mood with the harsh and awful facts of the death of Pauline Hanna, it was just another, perhaps extreme instance of the Polkinghorne trial exercising its fascination, drawing people in, providing something more serious than entertainment but very much resembling it.

We had to shout. I roared, 'I think it's so lovely that you've all kept in touch! That you've bonded over something so tragic!'

Jan yelled, 'I hope he wakes up every morning and thinks about what he's done and has terrible nightmares!'

'Do you think he has any redeeming qualities?'

'No!'

The music stopped. Robbyn leaned in, and said, 'I believe he's a raging narcissist, but he was clearly a brilliant surgeon. He saved a lot of people from going blind. I think there's a lot of patients who would be very, very grateful to him.'

I said, 'What do you think happened that night, Jan?'

She said, 'Well, we've all talked about it many times. I think she went to him and said, "I'm going to leave you. I'm taking half of everything and I'm going to expose you." And I reckon it was the thought of being exposed and the thought of her taking half his money that made him go into her bedroom, and I think she was probably asleep in a bed naked, maybe lying prone, face down. And I think he wrapped her up in a sheet and carried her over his shoulder because he's high on meth . . .'

I often took a book to the trial and one day was reading the John Updike short story 'The Other Woman'. It opens with a man going to the bathroom one night and noticing a piece of paper in an open drawer in his bedroom. It's a Valentine to his wife from another man. The discovery shocks him: 'The moon-struck snow outside the window seemed to leap bluely toward him, into him, with its smooth and expansive curves of coldness.' Had Pauline, too, made a shocking discovery that last night of her life, the moonlight leaping bluely through the curtains of her white house and into her bones already made cold by some revelation about her husband's life? This was the 'collision' theory

Alysha McClintock had put to the jury on Day 1, that his two lives, his two women, had collided, and his anger and frustration reached a terrible conclusion.

'Look,' I shouted, 'that's Ōrākei lagoon down there!' We all looked east at a small blue handkerchief of water. The music started up again. Robbyn shouted, 'You know, one of the things I kept looking at in the courtroom was his hands!'

'Whose hands?'

'Polkinghorne's hands!'

'Why were you looking at his hands!'

'Because,' she shouted, 'he did the finest eye surgery, and they looked so gentle!'

'I never really noticed that!'

She shouted something. I said, 'What?'

The music suddenly stopped, and she shouted so loudly that everyone in SkyBar could hear, 'But they were the same hands that strangled her to death!'

I didn't stay very long. I finished my drink and ate some peanuts, and we wished each other Merry Christmas, and a safe and happy New Year.

---

Nothing changed for the saddest person in courtroom 11, who took her seat in the public gallery every day but had next to nothing to do with the other court watchers, and had hardly any contact with anyone else, either. She wore smart clothes, a polished pair of black Doc Martens, and a backpack. She paced the High Court during recesses. One day just before the verdict, I saw her sitting by herself and staring straight ahead with wide eyes. I walked over and asked, 'Are you okay?'

She closed her eyes, and said, 'I come here every day to imitate having a nine-to-five job.'

This was the single most harrowing statement I heard during the entire trial. A person so lost, such an outcast, that they chose the High Court to come to every day to give the impression she was in regular employment. The Polkinghorne trial was beside the point. She took an interest in it, but it wasn't what attracted her to courtroom 11.

After the trial finished, I messaged her. 'How are things? Are you still up at the High Court sometimes? I hope you are getting some support. Life is hard isn't it. A bit of support from family or friends can go a long way.'

She replied, 'Still up there sometimes, yes. I'm not paid to be up there, and I don't want to encourage the powers that be to think that I'll go up there and watch them all being paid to work for free. So it is a bit difficult for me to know what to do, actually.

'Regarding support, it can go a long way, indeed. Unfortunately, things more seem to have worked out into a "with friends like these, who needs enemies?" kind of sort of a position. Where my supposed or apparent friends are not supportive of my goals or aims or aspirations. I get to thinking that maybe friends would be more likely to be found amongst the enemies of my frenemies, or similar. I don't quite know.

'I try and be good to myself. And I'm trying to be better about not being afraid of going solo or being by myself. Better to support myself with the things that I know than spend time with people who seem more interested in having me kept badly, indeed.'

Most or some of it was easy to follow, made sense; but she followed it up with a series of very long, incoherent messages, raving into space.

---

Nothing seemed real about a kind of sequel to the trial: a hearing to define the terms of an inquest into Pauline's death. A full inquest will be heard in August 2026.

On a lovely autumn morning in March 2025, a pre-inquest coroner's court conference was held at the Auckland District Court, that dismal old pile stinking up the downtown corner of Albert Street and Kingston Street. There was something a little bit juvenile, a little bit artificial about the hearing. Coroner Tania Tetitaha gave a karakia, and then she asked everyone to introduce themselves, 'So we can all get to know each other a little bit.' A little man in the back row stood up and said, 'My name is Philip Polkinghorne. I was married to Pauline Hanna.'

It was like a reunion. Everyone was there. There was Polkinghorne, dressed as per abnormally in mad socks of many colours. There was Crown prosecutor Alysha McClintock, and defence lawyer Ron Mansfield, and the same family members, the same mix of distinguished and undistinguished media, and the same trial addicts, The Polkinghorne Group, who took on a new, pious role: they were there, they stated, to support the family of Pauline Hanna. And there was the officer in charge, Detective Senior Sergeant Chris Allan, the ghost of failed murder investigations past. Polkinghorne ran into him outside the court and goaded him. 'Oh,' he said, 'I thought you'd be working at Countdown.'

The pre-inquest conference was held in the small confines of courtroom 8.2, on the freshly renovated eighth floor of the District Court. The polyester carpet was so new that it squeaked. The courtroom was windowless and clockless. Polkinghorne sat in the back row, beside his son, Taine. Pauline's family — her brother Bruce, his two children Jacob and Rose, and his wife Shelley — sat in the front row. Detective Senior Sergeant Chris Allan defied Polkinghorne's expectations he had been relegated to a supermarket checkout position by stating he continues to be in the employ of the New Zealand Police. As well as Crown and defence lawyers there was legal representation by court-appointed lawyers Simon Mount KC and Emma Finlayson-Davis.

That seemed to account for everyone, but a woman called out to the coroner: 'Excuse me, ma'am.' It was Tracey Hanna, Pauline's younger sister, appearing on video link from her home in England. I had missed her crucial appearance at the trial — she was the first witness for the defence, and claimed Pauline told her she had previously tried to die by suicide — and I didn't recognise the woman on screen wearing a smile that was at once serene and rigidly fixed onto her face.

The purpose of the pre-inquest conference was to establish whether there was support for a formal inquest. The Crown said they supported it. The defence said they saw a need for it, too. Tracey agreed, as did Taine Polkinghorne. The coroner was about to move on, but Bruce Hanna called out, 'I support it.' Coroner Tetitaha said, 'I figured you would, but I should have asked you. Thank you, Mr Hanna.'

Behold, then, just about the first and only time in the whole weird, sorry saga of the death of Pauline Hanna and the murder-accused Dr Philip Polkinghorne, that everyone agreed on something. Everyone was on the same page, everyone wished to see the day when the death of Pauline Hanna would be ruled upon in an inquest. Coroner Tetitaha set the August 2026 date. She said her focus was purely on the cause and circumstances of Pauline's death. 'The issue will be how it occurred,' she said. 'My interest is what happened on the night.'

Yes, that's quite an interesting subject. 'This death involves a suspected self-inflicted death,' the coroner noted in a minute. That was an elegant way of putting it.

---

Nothing left, now, except Polkinghorne. Last man standing, the deranged sex goblin in situ, at the house of horrors itself, 121 Upland Road above Ōrākei Basin, the water turned black on a summer's day as a storm rolled in — visitors talked of him opening the massive front door in January 2025, a tiny, tightly muscled man in his seventy-second year, alone in the house where Pauline lived and died.

The following chapter is a re-creation of what was said and observed by knowledgeable parties in the Polkinghorne home. The following chapter is the inside story of what his life is like after all that happened. The following chapter is up close and personal with Polkinghorne — and Polkinghorne's terrifying mini-me.

CHAPTER 13

# At Home with Polkinghorne

He was not actually alone in the house. He had a constant companion. It followed him everywhere. 'Down, Winston!' he commanded, feebly, to the bulldog that he bought in Pauline's honour — on the date of her birthday and a year after her death — because she always wanted a bulldog, but did she or anyone want a bulldog like this? What an awful creature it was, jumping up and snuffling and licking its stupid chops, its bark like a loud sneeze, so disconsolate at a few seconds' lack of attention that it set up a horrible whining.

'Down!'

Winston had identifiably narcissistic tendencies.

'Stop that!'

Winston had a squashed and ugly face.

'Down!'

His visitor — an interested party, let's say, for the purposes of this tale: there were certain stipulations about relaying what took place that day — was shown into an empty house. Polkinghorne was getting it ready for sale. The kitchen was bare except for dog biscuits and packets of French Earl Grey tea. He had already boxed his beloved encyclopaedias and atlases and was packing up other books to dump — here, he said to the guest, take this if you like, and gave away a copy of his hardbacked 2007 thesis *Rhegmatogenous Retinal Detachment: A New Zealand Perspective*. 'I remain deeply indebted,' he writes in the acknowledgements page, 'for the support of my wife, Pauline Hanna, who has really made this achievement possible.'

He made tea. He bade the visitor sit at the dining-room table. One of the white chairs was used by Pauline, in his version of events, to hang herself on; he took his guest to where she died, on a small landing by a side door. He did so quite chattily. He talked about how he had told police he got up that morning to make tea and toast, and 'for some reason' had walked across to the other side of the house, where he found Pauline hanging. He remembered what that reason was: to feed the cats. Their bowls were near the side door.

This was a vital piece of evidence to the defence case, but it was forever being mocked, and shut down, whenever the subject came up at the trial. Harrison Smith tried asking a witness about the cat bowls. 'I'm not really sure what the relevance of the cat bowl is,' Justice Graham Lang said. Smith tried telling him the relevance, that it explained how it was Polkinghorne found Pauline's body, but the judge chose one of the few times in the entire trial to assert himself and cut him off. Later, in her closing address, Crown prosecutor Alysha McClintock made the sarcastic remark, 'The answer's not in the cat bowls, I can tell you that.'

Polkinghorne continued his tour of the house. He showed the interested party Pauline's bedroom. Then he walked across the hall, and showed his guest his bedroom, where he slept on the night she died. The two bedrooms were a long way apart, he pointed out, and that was why he hadn't heard anything that night, not Pauline getting up to find a rope, not Pauline positioning one of the white chairs from the dining room, not Pauline hanging herself. Fast asleep the whole time in a distant bedroom. Slept like a baby. As ever, and still very much the case, he claimed he slept the sleep of an innocent.

And that was his whole theme, his entire being, as presented to his guest that day — he was innocent of everything, first and obviously foremost of killing his wife, but he also denied ever strangling Pauline the way that Pheasant and John Riordan had testified she had told them one night over dinner, and, despite his guilty plea, he also resolutely denied possessing methamphetamine. He said it wasn't his. He said he didn't buy it. He had probably, he told his guest, who was served tea in the same white dining-room chair that may have been used by Pauline when she died, only ever taken methamphetamine between four and ten times in his life. It was a casual thing, like smoking marijuana. He didn't actually enjoy it very much. The interested party did not know what to say to that and drank the tea too quickly for something to do. Polkinghorne continued that it didn't make him feel euphoric; it merely kept him alert. He said he couldn't see the point of being awake all night. He'd rather be asleep, sleeping the sleep of the innocent . . . Asked, then, to whom the enormous 37.7-gram stash of methamphetamine belonged to, he answered that: a) the cops planted a fair bit of it, and brought out photos to back up his assertion and b) it was Pauline's. The visitor asked, trying not to let on that the scalding-hot tea had possibly caused permanent damage, 'Are you saying Pauline bought it?' He said she *acquired* it.

French Earl Grey has a beautiful perfume. The visitor talked of going to see Polkinghorne with an open mind about the death of Pauline. They felt for Polkinghorne, appreciated that he saw himself as persecuted, a pariah. They did not wish to judge. A jury had declared him not guilty. Perhaps it was as simple and sad as Pauline's family not being able to accept that she hanged herself. But the visitor began to find something unpleasant and cloying in the perfumed tea as Polkinghorne continued to present himself as an entirely blameless and ambushed bystander who got caught up in the affairs and lies of others. It was one thing to approach him with an open mind and another thing to find him plausible. In the documentary series *Polk*, he came across as unreliable and gross; it wasn't so much what he said as what he did with his mouth, the way he twisted his lips whenever he finished a sentence.

'Down!'

Winston was determined to get at the date scones Polkinghorne had put out.

'No!'

Winston was unstoppable, insatiable.

'Hey! No!'

The guest saw that Polkinghorne had printed out a chapter on the book he was writing. It lay on the table. It dealt with the ESR testing conducted at his house, and damned it as incompetent. But the chapter was quite unreadable, a densely concentrated scientific paper in a similar style, without the learned footnotes and patient reckoning, of his 2007 masterpiece *Rhegmatogenous Retinal Detachment*. It included photos of the steps where he claimed he fell and banged his head when he was helping Pauline's body off the chair.

The steps were part of the guided tour he gave to his visitor. Relaying what it was like to visit Chez Polk, the visitor mentioned afterwards how strange it was to stand there and stare at these steps in the knowledge that they were likely the most mocked steps in New Zealand criminal justice; Crown prosecutor Brian Dickey had all but laughed out loud in court when he cross-examined the expert witness who said he had detected Polkinghorne's blood. 'It was planted, wasn't it,' Dickey had said, disgustedly.

If Polkinghorne had elected to give evidence — and it was my understanding that it was a very late call not to do so, a decision only made right up to the last minute — then Dickey would surely have gone at him, aggressively and mockingly, probably right from the opening question, and asked him how he killed his wife. He would have said to him that it wasn't very hard, was it, that he knew exactly what to do, how to avoid causing her defensive injuries by putting her in a sleeper hold, which arteries to put pressure on, that it would only have taken five or six seconds to knock her out, that he may not have been a very tall man but very strong, physically fit, and she was very slight as well as sedated by wine and zopiclone . . . The robust cross-examination would have set out to take away the very thing the Crown believed was at the root of Polkinghorne's strength: control. His frustration might have come out in a display of the very thing the Crown believed was at the root of Polkinghorne's failure: anger.

Every book is a little intricate universe that the author wishes to control. Polkinghorne's work in progress was his ordering of events, his testament to his innocence. He wanted to get it right in his head. He was working very hard on it, accessing information that wasn't presented in court, such as police disclosures and private texts, too, between himself and Madison Ashton.

There was her name, said out loud, by the man who supposedly killed for her, to be with her, to 'fuck her endlessly' as he texted her. Polkinghorne's visitor felt emboldened to ask about Madison. Polkinghorne was quite happy to answer their questions. The guest observed his response as classic Polkinghorne. Ask him something, and he will ramble on and on, just as he had in his epic police interview on the day of Pauline's death, sometimes incoherently, never in a linear or rational manner, always assuming the role he had fashioned for himself in the entire saga of hookers and meth and death: a victim.

---

It was Polkinghorne's opinion that Madison was working for the police from day one. He meant their famous rendezvous at Mount Cook. (He told his guest with an impish grin that when the cops knocked on the door of their chalet, he said to them, cool as a cucumber, 'We've been expecting you.') Yes, yes, he agreed, it was a terrible decision to meet her there. But it was just a spontaneous thing. She said to him, 'You've just gotta get out of Auckland. I'll look after you.' So down he travelled, and little did he know, as he put it, that it was a poisoned chalice.

He was right about it being a poisoned chalice, a PR disaster, but the rest of the story seemed entirely disingenuous — that it wasn't his idea to go to Mount Cook, that his indecent haste to go to Mount Cook (only 25 days after Pauline had died) wasn't about his need to have sex with Madison, that the only reason he decided to go to Mount Cook was because he needed someone, anyone, to help him cope with the tragic loss of his beloved wife. So what that it happened to be Madison, his sex worker of fevered choice? The guest asked him outright if he had been in love with her, and he said that he was, at times. That was nice. That was normal. Of course he could not leave it at that. He added that if Adolf Hitler was in a life raft at that time, he would have taken his hand. Madison Ashton relegated to Adolf fucking Hitler. He could be so loveless, so cruel, an unfeeling little toad lording it over an empty home above a lagoon.

Sometimes the visitor wondered whether anything had any meaning to Polkinghorne. Asked whether he lied to Madison when he'd told her that he had left Pauline and she no longer lived at their house, he said he probably did, but only because she was nagging him to get married.

He picked up the subject later, when he talked about attending counselling sessions with Madison. He described how Madison spent the first twenty minutes going on and on about what a terrible person he was; she was talking over him the whole time, it was intolerable, just awful — so, yes, returning to the issue of whether he told Madison the lie that Pauline had left their house and their marriage, he claimed he would have said yes just to shut her up. That was the thing with Madison. She would just. Never. Shut. Up.

Neither would Winston.

'Stop that!

He whined and sneezed, shrieked and burped.

'Hey!'

The sour tea, the hard date scone, the empty house . . . A woman — poor, lonely Pauline — died here. Another woman — poor, lonely Madison — called here, on FaceTime. It was a haunted house. The ghosts of the two women trod the stairs, looked upon the little man with impressive biceps in a pink shirt and shorts, going about his business, free as a bird on a summer's morning. The guest asked him, 'Do you miss her?'

Polkinghorne replied that he felt sorry for Madison more than anything, even to this day. He was sorry that she didn't have any friends.

'Were you a friend?' the guest asked, uncharacteristically forward, but there was something in Polkinghorne's manner that invited it: as if he wanted to confide; had been alone with his thoughts too long.

Polkinghorne had definitely seen himself as a friend and in fact went on to cast himself as a very noble friend. He talked about how supportive he had been to Madison. For example, he claimed she had a breast implant that went wrong — one breast pointed one way and the other pointed another. She had them redone and picked up a bad infection. It was all very stressful and he was there for her at times like that, steadfast and true. What a great guy, notwithstanding his mocking description of her surgery — he mimed one breast west, one breast east.

As for the counselling sessions, he deflected the idea they were to maintain a relationship. He didn't see it that they were even really *in* a relationship. So what was the goal? He wasn't sure. Maybe, he reflected, that it was to repair a friendship . . . He even likened it to a workplace issue. Sometimes work colleagues reached an impasse and had to seek arbitration. His guest shifted uncomfortably in their seat. It was like that, he maintained. You work with someone, but a problem arises and it needs to be fixed so that you can continue to work together . . .

The visitor recoiled at the distancing Polkinghorne attempted — stripping away his intense, heavily sexual relationship with Madison and likening her to a platonic work colleague. It was a kind of dehumanising. Definitely it was insulting. He talked about her as someone who was simply out to get him, a friendless harridan, anxious and insecure, who wouldn't shut up.

The visitor said they sat there and thought back to the trial, when very, very many texts and other messages between Polkinghorne and Madison were read out in court. They established how much he wanted her, desired her, needed her. And so the guest said, 'Without Madison, the cops may not have even pursued the whole thing. Because that's the simple arithmetic, isn't it? Their equation was, "This man has killed his wife to be with this woman." That's it. That's it in a nutshell.'

Polkinghorne pointed out that this was describing a motive. But before you get to the motive, there has to be evidence of homicide. And there was none. That was where the cops made their crucial mistake. They were so obsessed with Madison

Ashton as the highly sexualised motive that they missed what happened.

That was it. For all the sex workers, however much they cost, for all of the obvious attractions of Madison and his desire to see her, and for all the impression that Polkinghorne sometimes gave of being callous, mean, someone really quite odious and self-serving, the proof that Pauline had been killed was absent, missing, not adding up; that was it in a nutshell. His guest had to acknowledge the truth of that basic premise. It felt fundamentally wrong to sit there and judge him harshly. The temptation was to fall into line with the police, the Crown, Pauline's family, Pauline's friends, Pauline's work colleagues, and with the vast majority of people who followed the trial and view him as a murderer who lied about everything. But where was the evidence? The jury had got it right. He deserved to come home. His fate was Winston.

---

Justice had been done. But would he ever find peace? The guest described him as anxious and obsessive, reliving the trial and his treatment, putting it down on paper, writing up to twenty drafts of each unreadable chapter, remembering small things like the names he came up with for key figures such as police investigation head Chris Allan (Crooked Chris) and ESR scientist Fiona Matheson (Filthy Fiona), seizing on pieces of evidence such as urine on Pauline's dressing gown suggesting she was seated when she died, attacking the police who ought to have known *immediately* that Pauline had not died by homicide but instead rushed to get the wrong end of the stick and treated him abominably, like taking him from the house that day and placing him in the back of a locked police car for fifteen minutes simply to fuck with his head . . . Yes, he acknowledged, he was bitter. Of course he was. He was an innocent man dragged through Hell.

Critics of the verdict, and the whole process of Polkinghorne being able to afford the expert services of Ron Mansfield, made pious noises about white privilege. But the issue was taken up and turned on its head by Polkinghorne himself, who talked about how lucky he was to be able to afford it, and that the average person didn't have a dog's show of getting a robust and thorough defence. The system was unfair. The fact that it worked to his advantage illuminated how others were disadvantaged. As for the actual cost, he put a figure on it when asked by insiders. Ron Mansfield's services had cost him between two and three million dollars.

The fees are ongoing. An inquest into Pauline's death is scheduled for August 2026. Polkinghorne welcomed it. His thinking was that if the coroner came out with a verdict of unexplained death rather than suicide, that was all to the good, because it left the door open to the very thing that killed her.

The guest asked him, 'What do you think was the cause of death?'

He thought that she went up to bed on the last night of her life, developed post-vaccine encephalitis from her Covid shot, and went mad.

God almighty. Really? Had he sunk so low that he descended to the alternative thinking of the anti-vax ferals? The theory even managed to silence the appalling Winston. On that occasion the dog slept quietly at Polkinghorne's feet.

What can be said in favour of the idea that Pauline died as a result of the Covid vaccine? Encephalitis is an inflammatory condition of the brain that has been described as a severe neurological complication of Covid. It led to a study in South Korea. The research team wrote, 'We sought to evaluate the risk of encephalitis and meningitis after Covid-19 vaccination in the entire South Korean population [. . .] Our findings suggest an overall increased risk of encephalitis after vaccination. However, the absolute risk was small and should not impede vaccine confidence.' Small, but present . . . It was, then, within the realms of possibility, but at the extreme edge of that realm. Mansfield shot it down as a defence tactic before trial. He knew it ran the risk of making the defence look ridiculous.

Mansfield didn't want a bar of another theory that Polkinghorne thought might have been worth looking into: that she died of autoerotic misadventure. A sex game gone wrong. The notion that a belt and a rope attached to her neck, while sitting in a chair on a downstairs landing, would be really exciting, might make her achieve the orgasm of a lifetime or whatever . . . This belonged to the impression of Pauline that Polkinghorne had tried on with Pauline's friend Alison Ring, who told the jury that he had visited her just after the tragedy, and said to her, offensively and charmlessly, ' She wouldn't just fuck one man. She'd fuck the whole team.' Pauline, always up for it, so mad for it that she'd go to any lengths — they were vile presentations for her family to have to deal with, and Polkinghorne has continued to portray her in that way. Insiders talked of Polkinghorne saying that he wasn't the only one in his marriage who indulged an avid consumption of sex workers. Pauline was in on it, too. They had a male sex worker set to give evidence. Oh and she didn't just have one vibrator in her bedside drawer, he said with pursed lips. She had three or four — a team of them.

Mansfield didn't go there and neither did he go near Polkinghorne's assertion that the methamphetamine belonged to Pauline: 'If you've got a library book in your house from Auckland City Library, then it's in your possession,' he told his client, by way of analogy. They argued about whether he should enter a guilty plea. In the end Polkinghorne gave in, but he maintained his innocence even after the verdict and before his sentence for drug possession, telling a pre-sentence report writer that Pauline had bought the meth. Justice Graham Lang said at sentencing, 'I do not accept that assertion . . . I am satisfied you were the owner and the purchaser of the methamphetamine.' Carolyne Meng-Yee reported in the *Herald* that she spoke with a drug dealer who sold Polkinghorne 56 grams of methamphetamine for $14,000.

None of it made any difference to Polkinghorne. He stuck to his story, told his truth. The visitor who met him over date scones and tea said that he described Pauline as a wild spirit, a beautiful, wonderful, loving woman, capable of anything. But his rhapsodies went only so far, and he began listing some of the things about her which annoyed the hell out of him. She had a lot of make-up and crap like that; she'd lug it around the house, and the shower was full of every known thing to man or beast. He brought up the cold and heartless letter he wrote to her in 2018 that was read out in court, and he repeated his complaints that she never paid any of the bills, that he even had to sort out her unpaid parking fines at Middlemore Hospital.

The interested party asked, 'Were you still in love with her?'

He claimed he was, and that they had got back on track in the last twelve months of her life. They started to talk about retirement. They were looking forward to growing old together. It was all going to be great. Nothing seemed out of place on the last night of her life. They had a couple of glasses of wine in the upstairs library. She cooked pork strips with broccoli. She also baked potatoes, but for some reason they forgot to eat them. They watched TV. He didn't think anything was any different from any other night. Madness — maybe hers, maybe his — came out of nowhere.

---

'Winston!'

The beast was at it again, leaping at a guest.

'Don't jump up!'

It jumped up.

'It's very rude!'

Polkinghorne had sold a McCahon painting towards Mansfield's fees, but he still held on to a Hotere. The walls were otherwise bare. An ironing board was set up in Pauline's bedroom. Downstairs, a little framed oval photo of Polkinghorne and Pauline was propped up on the kitchen bench. He spent more of his time at his beach home in the Coromandel and one of his activities back in Remuera in the summer of 2025 was to box up his possessions to get the house ready for sale — not for the first time. There had been no takers in previous efforts. Any house sale includes the question in disclosures, 'Is the vendor aware of any incident of unnatural death or violent crime (e.g. suicide, murder) at the property?'

He told his visitor that the neighbours were all good with his return to the house. But — he darkened — as for his old workmates at Auckland Eye, the staff there, some he'd worked with for over twenty years, not one of them, *none*, without exception, had put out a hand. He seemed surprised. All the claims of his use of methamphetamine at work had been rubbished in court, he said. Not a word of truth in it. The guilty party was most likely a seventeen-year-old patient. But where were his colleagues? They had dived for cover, were nowhere to be seen; he was treated better by a security guard at the trial, who told Polkinghorne, 'You'll walk.' The kindness of strangers . . . As well, he reassured his guest, as a fantastic network of old friends who stayed with him all the way through.

It was natural for everyone to feel deep sympathy for Pauline. It felt unnatural to feel anything resembling sympathy for Polkinghorne, but his private life had been paraded in front of the nation, he'd suffered the trauma of losing his wife and then being accused of killing her — according to the visitor, Polkinghorne hinted he was in counselling, was getting help. He made references to a persecution complex, to sitting around feeling okay and then suddenly something would hit him. He was anxious the police would pull some other, new stunt and produce a woman from his past and accuse him of rape. He had nothing to hide, but his concern was that the police wouldn't ever roll over. They hadn't finished with him. They'd never give up . . .

Polkinghorne, a paranoid obsessive, shuffling around the empty house with his barking, crazed shadow, denying everything they threw at him — the Riordans were pissed as parrots that night over dinner when Pauline claimed he strangled her; that was absolute bullshit, he never laid a hand on her. And so he bent his head to the task of writing it all down. It was therapeutic. He was getting better. The first year after Pauline died, he went absolutely crazy and had two suicide attempts. He tried to gas himself in his car and he also tried taking his own life at his sister Ruth's house. How? He couldn't remember.

The visitor was concerned, unnerved. Polkinghorne was asked, 'What — did you take an overdose of pills?'

He shook his head and described that as a waste of time. You're never going to die on pills, he said, neatly heading off all the people who claimed Pauline would never have chosen hanging as a way to end her life, that she would have taken an overdose of the many, many pills in her possession.

Persecuted, suicidal, stuck with Winston — surely, maybe, potentially, a little bit of sympathy for the devil of Remuera was due? He had faced trial, faced the music. He was found not guilty. He was sentenced to 150 hours for methamphetamine possession and got through it in the first month. He had wanted to work it off in a food bank, but he was told that wasn't an option.

Once the house was sold, he wasn't going to head for the hills or take up a new life in Australia or elsewhere; his intention was to stay in Auckland, closer to his sister Ruth. He loves Auckland. He has no intention of leaving. He goes to the gym, he translates medical texts from French and German into English, he gardens in the Coromandel house, he walks the damned dog. Ruth had given him two pieces of advice after the verdict: 'Get a garden and get a dog.' He did as he was advised. And so it had come to this, on a humid morning in January, a storm coming in and Dr Philip Polkinghorne stacking two cups and two plates in the sink. He showed his guest out. There was the flash of a smile at the front door. He looked smaller than ever. He used to tell Pauline that she treated him like the doll she never had as a child; she chose all his clothes, laid them out every morning before he went to work. He pulled at the pink shirt and pair of shorts. Pauline had picked them out for him. He told his visitor he was blessed until the day she died.

And so the guest said goodbye and left Polkinghorne to get on with his day, to carry on being Polkinghorne, that tiny creature of mood and whim, found not guilty of the murder of his wife, free to do as he pleased.

The guest asked him outright, 'Phil, did you kill Pauline?'

Not a chance, he said. Not a chance. No.

'Have you got a new partner?'

Oh hell no, he said. No. No way. Who, he said, would have him? They'd be murdered in a minute, wouldn't they, he said. Because, he said, he knew how to commit the perfect murder. Polkinghorne, famous for his black humour; Polkinghorne, who was only joking; Polkinghorne, who had the last laugh.

# Acknowledgements

Allen & Unwin are my sixth publisher over fourteen books and although not in the same class as Luncheon Sausage Books they have been a joy to deal with, and I am grateful to all their staff but especially publisher Michelle Hurley, who talked me into writing the book without ever seeming to talk me into writing the book to the point where I was really hoping she would come straight out and talk me into writing the book. I am grateful for her warmth, trust and very fine professional care. Many thanks also to project editor Leonie Freeman and the book's designer, Katrina Duncan, who I have known all her life as her uncle and have never ceased to be amazed at her sense of style. I am grateful also to editor Emma Neale, whose lively intelligence and encouragement of a good sentence made her the flat-out best editor I have worked with in publishing.

I need to thank numerous people at source — that is, during the trial of Dr Philip Polkinghorne. First and foremost are *The New Zealand Herald* reporters Carolyne Meng-Yee and

George Block. We spent a lot of time together and I could not wish for better or more inspiring company. Thanks also to *Herald* news editor Tom Dillane, who kept a close watch on the often potentially libellous stories I filed throughout the trial and to this day does not know how we got away with it. Thanks are due to NZME for copyright permission, and to my outstanding former colleagues Jared Savage, Nick Jones, Craig Kapitan, Isaac Davison, Simon Wilson, Katie Harris and Shayne Currie. I miss them. I also wish to thank other media who covered the trial, primarily the world-class Catrin Owen from *Stuff*, and film-maker Mark McNeill, who produced a sensitive and dramatic record of the trial in his three programmes for Discovery. His series thanked the Hanna family, Pauline Hanna's best friend Pheasant Riordan, and Madison Ashton for their involvement, as do I for their time and patience during and after the trial. They are lovely people.

Mark's series did not thank Philip Polkinghorne. I wish to thank him sincerely. I also thank prosecutors Alysha McClintock and Brian Dickey, defence lawyers Ron Mansfield and Harrison Smith, and Craig Cartwright, to my mind, the sole representative from the New Zealand Police of merit during the trial. The gang of trial watchers who took their seats in the public gallery most days were not there in any official capacity but I hereby officially thank Jan Naish-Wallis of Howick, Francine Cameron of Grey Lynn, Lois Osborne of Whangārei and Robbyn Storey of Raglan for the soundtrack of horror and fascination that they provided. Their cult also included my old friend Steven O'Meagher, who I always look up to for his high spirits and sense of cool. The High Court of Auckland is a weird and absorbing castle of justice. I am grateful to have a life outside its walls, and wish to acknowledge the love and support of Tayi Tibble, Finlay Macdonald, Carol Hirschfeld, Shayne Carter, Gary Steel, Megan Nicol Reed, Colleen Maria Lenihan, Stacy Gregg and, of course, last and forever first, Minka Braunias.

# About the author

Steve Braunias is the author of fourteen books, including *Fool's Paradise* (Random House, winner of the best first book of nonfiction at the 2002 national book awards), *Civilisation* (Awa Press, winner of the best book of non-fiction at the 2013 national book awards), *Missing Persons* (HarperCollins, winner of the non-fiction prize for crime writing at the 2023 Ngaio Marsh awards) and *The Man Who Ate Lincoln Road* (Luncheon Sausage Books, 2017). He serves as the literary editor at *Newsroom* and writes a fortnightly column for the *Listener*. He lives in Herne Bay.